PRAISE FOR THE

Curious Encounters of the Human Kind

SERIES

"Most of Paul Sochaczewski's curious encounters start out as intelligent travel writing, exploring hidden corners of Asia and characters very much out of the ordinary. But this series works on a more complex level: he frequently zooms in and out of left field with a curious tangent, a sensitive reminiscence, a provocative opinion, a new way of looking at events that already are beyond most 'normal' travelers' tales. I read each story feeling refreshed, enlightened, and curious to see what the next stage of Sochaczewski's journey would bring."

—JUDITH M. HEIMANN, author of *The Most Offending Soul Alive: Tom Harrisson and His Remarkable Life* and *The Airmen and the Headhunters: A True Story of Lost Soldiers, Heroic Tribesmen and the Unlikeliest Rescue of World War II*

"What a discovery! Paul Sochaczewski is that rarest of writers who knows that the real 'Asian miracle' isn't malls or computer geeks. In his years traveling the continent, he has discovered an eternal assemblage of arcane explorers, putative emperors, frivolous mystics, sacrosanct elephants and, yes, miracle workers. When Sochaczewski finds them, in Javanese palaces or sacred forests protected by spirits, they are caviar (or sweetened bird's nest) for his fascinating portraits. A book for everyone who knows that the Mysterious East is alive and well, and more how-about-that-wonderful than you perhaps imagined."

—HARRY ROLNICK, author of *The Chinese Gourmet, The Complete Book of Coffee,* and *Spice Chronicles: Exotic Tales of a Hungry Traveler*

"Paul Sochaczewski skips about Asia like a Monkey God hopping from mountain to mountain, bringing back life-prolonging peaches while annoying the gatekeepers. Whatever you do, follow him on this journey!"

—LEE CHOR LIN, director of the National Museum of Singapore; former curator of Asian Civilizations Museum – Singapore; author of *Batik: Creating an Identity*

"Sochaczewski is a world-class searcher, reporter, and observer who has criss-crossed Asia for forty years, pausing in the most unlikely places and finding extraordinary people. The essays in this insightful and witty chronicle present a rich tapestry of eccentric nobles, self-serving naturalists, scoundrels who will make your teeth ache, celebrity monks, and memorable folks whose stories are too good to be true. But they are."

—CHRISTOPHER G. MOORE, author of the Vincent Calvino novels and *Heart Talk*

"In this series Sochaczewski explores the hidden corners, the forgotten people, and their surprising tales. All the personal traveler's tales in these volumes are captivating, all filled with humor, drama, and insight, with an edgy take-no-prisoners voice. You won't find anything else like this on the bookshelf."

—JEFF MCNEELY, chief scientist, International Union for Conservation of Nature

"The *Curious Encounters of the Human Kind* series is a delicious stew of improbable characters and intriguing stories, served up in thoroughly pithy style, and with a hearty dash of irreverent humour."

—TIM HANNIGAN, author of *Raffles and the British Invasion of Java* and *Brief History of Indonesia: Sultans, Spices, and Tsunamis: The Incredible Story of Southeast Asia's Largest Nation*

"Constructed on a base of strange but true personal travel adventures, *Curious Encounters* adds elements of history, an edgy sense of humour, mysticism, political incorrectness, current affairs, and memorable characters you'll wish you had the pleasure to meet on your travels. Consider each book in this series like a good curry – the result is more than the sum of its parts; each tale has its own zing. Travel with these books to the little-visited corners of Asia, and savour them.

—JASON BROOKE, director of The Brooke Trust

"I never tire of living vicariously through Paul Sochaczewski and his writing adventures. He keeps finding these wonderful details that miraculously open up entire worlds to be explored. Paul is the last of the Great Hunters, only instead of trophies, it is stories he brings home for our admiration, wonder, and delight."

—MARK OLSHAKER, Emmy-winning filmmaker; author of *Einstein's Brain*, *The Edge*, and *Mindhunter*

"The *Curious Encounters* series is proof positive that a writer/traveler can immerse himself in Asian cultures and yet remain objective enough to write extremely entertaining and often irreverent articles and colorful stories about what he has experienced. From Indonesian mystics to Burmese white elephant hunters, the descriptions are spot-on. There is something in these articles and stories that reminds me of the writing of Paul Theroux – not as cynical, perhaps, but the author is just as able to look at events with a clear, unsentimental and yet sympathetic eye. You won't regret a moment spent reading these tales, which perfectly capture the allure and spice of the places visited."

—DEAN BARRETT, author of *Memoirs of a Bangkok Warrior*

CURIOUS ENCOUNTERS
of the
HUMAN KIND

INDONESIA

CURIOUS

ENCOUNTERS

of the

HUMAN KIND

INDONESIA

*True Asian Tales of
Folly, Greed, Ambition
and Dreams*

PAUL SPENCER SOCHACZEWSKI

EXPLORER'S EYE PRESS

GENEVA, SWITZERLAND

Cover photo: Young girl in Kampong Rangko in Flores, near where Hobbits are found.

All photos by Paul Sochaczewski, except where noted. Jeffrey McNeely contributed to an earlier version of "Searching for Small Folk at the End of the Trail."

ISBN: 978-2-940573-04-2

Published by:
Explorer's Eye Press
Geneva, Switzerland

Book design by Stacey Aaronson
Map of Indonesia by John Welding

Printed in the United States of America

Dedicated to the people of Asia who shared their stories, and sometimes their homes, rice wine, termite omelets, and dreams.

TABLE OF CONTENTS

AUTHOR'S NOTE

Some thoughts about change in Indonesia:

Roll out the superlatives – the world's largest archipelago, both in number of islands (nobody is quite sure how many, but seventeen thousand plus is a starting point), breadth (distance similar to Seattle to Boston or London to Tehran), and population (the world's fourth most populous country, after the USA). It has the world's largest Muslim population but is not an Islamic state. The island of Java has the highest population density of any large land area on the planet, with many of those people living within sight of an active volcano. It's one of the world's most biologically and culturally diverse countries.

On the international stage, Indonesia has only infrequently explored its potential muscle; that might change as the country tries to base its foreign policy on its historical maritime influence.

Indonesia shouldn't really exist as a single country. There are just too many ethnic groups, languages, religions, and cultures spread over too vast an area to form a homogenous whole.

Yet the people of Indonesia have, for the most part, bought into the nationalistic spirit, all the while retaining strong local identities.

One major change has been the growth of a middle class, a by-product of increased healthcare, improved education, and access to global communications. When I first started working in Indonesia in 1971, a few people were wealthy and most people were anything but. In intervening years an informed, active middle class has evolved, with men and women as eager to consume resources and manufactured goods as their counterparts elsewhere in the world. And they talk to each other incessantly; Indonesians are the world's greatest users of social media.

It's an improbable country, with an easy-to-learn language that is pronounced just as it's written, with grammar so simple even I learned it.

It's got depth – layers of beliefs and behaviors with linguistic, historical, and cultural complexities that somehow create a country that is more than the sum of its parts.

And, of course, it's got problems. Environmental destruction, corruption (enhanced by decentralization), and an ingrained reluctance to complete projects on schedule, on budget, and with quality control.

It works on its own terms. And yet, Indonesia is my favorite country in Southeast Asia. Perhaps because no matter how long I stay there and how sanguine I feel that I've figured things out, something socks me in the jaw and I realize I have no idea what's going on. Maybe because I have family and friends all over the country. Maybe it's because of the spirits that inhabit the sputtering volcanoes.

Some of these chapters were written, in simpler forms, over a period of several decades. While in some cases statistics might have changed in recent years, the basic truth of the human stories offered here of foibles, ambitions, and achievements remains constant.

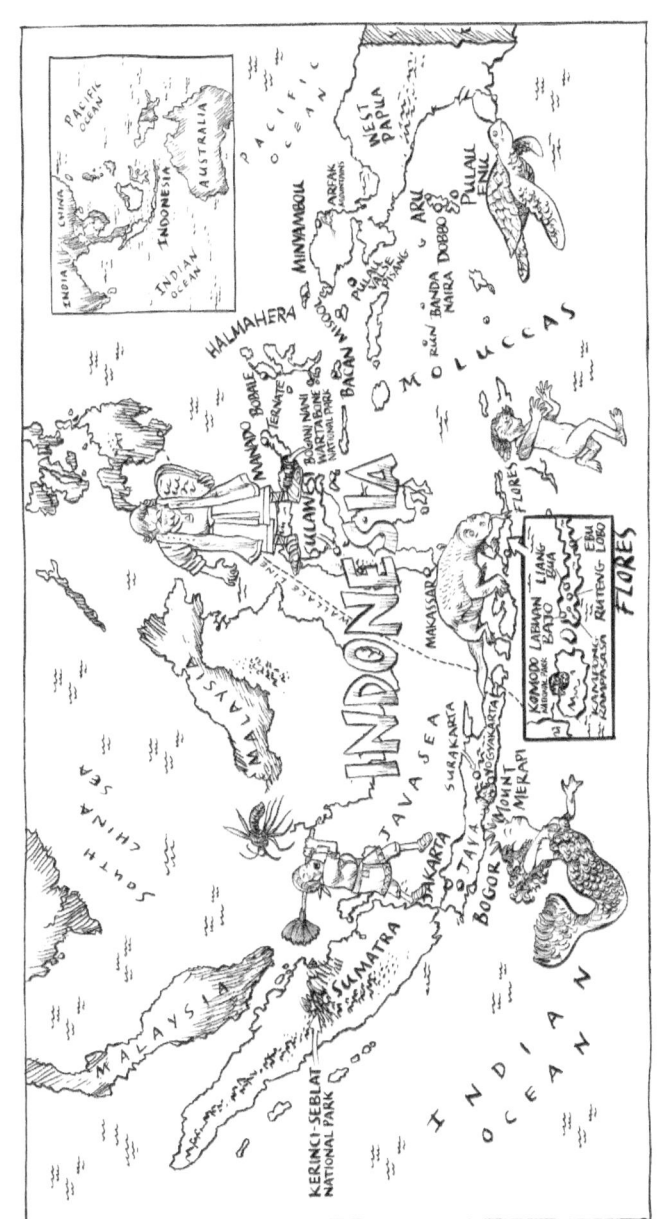

Wuri, a young woman from Surakarta, dances the *bedoyo ketawang*. "Switch modes" and you might see a tenth dancer. That would be the Mermaid Queen.

THE SULTAN AND THE MERMAID QUEEN:

A LOVE STORY FOR THE AGES

Some relationships aren't meant to be analyzed too closely.
"Accept it. Or not."

SURAKARTA, JAVA

The instructions, given by a friend of Javanese nobility, were tantalizingly vague. If you look really carefully, and if the wind is blowing right and you are of good heart and you let yourself "switch mode" into a semi-trance, you just might see a tenth dancer. That would be the Queen herself.

My friend was referring to the *bedoyo ketawang*, a sacred court dance held once a year in August, in honor of the ongoing love affair between the kings of Java and Kanjeng Ratu Kidul, a mermaid-like spirit who is considered the Queen of the Southern Ocean. In this ninety-minute performance, nine virgins weave an intricate and highly stylized ritual in front of the current king of Surakarta, Susuhunan Paku Buwono XIII. If a tenth dancer is seen, palace watchers say, that blink-of-an-eye appearance would be the Mermaid Queen herself, come to pay her respects and reaffirm her love for the monarch.

Through my friend's intercession, my wife and I were invited to witness this dance, which is not open to the public. We thought it would be a perfectly suitable honeymoon event, more memorable than the Elvis impersonators of Las Vegas, more romantic than the canals of Venice.

The *bedoyo ketawang* reflects one of Asia's most magical *histoires d'amour* – the affair between Panembahan Senopati, a late sixteenth-century king of Java, and Kanjeng Ratu Kidul, a princess who was turned into a mermaid goddess. Together, this unlikely couple began one of the world's longest surviving regal lines – the royal families of Yogyakarta and Surakarta, in central Java, Indonesia.

IN ONE OF MANY VERSIONS OF THE MYTH, A BEAUTIFUL princess from the Padjajaran kingdom was afflicted by leprosy as a result of a curse inflicted by her jealous stepmother. In this disfigured state she brought shame to the kingdom, and in despair the unfortunate young woman went to Java's raging southern coast to meditate, where a divine voice enticed her to enter the ocean and become reborn as a beautiful aquatic queen.

Meanwhile, Senopati, a very real Javanese ruler, was having his own *crise de coeur* and he too headed south for prayer and contemplation. While sitting on a rock on the dramatic sea cliffs south of Yogyakarta, Senopati was lured into the ocean by the spirit who became known as Kanjeng Ratu Kidul, the Queen of the Southern Ocean. During their three-day honeymoon bacchanal in her submerged palace, she taught him the secrets of love and the intricacies of good governance.

Kanjeng Ratu Kidul promised to be the consort for all of Senopati's descendants. All great kings benefit from a spiritual connection; in central Java that divine guidance is provided by Kanjeng Ratu Kidul.

A BIT OF EXPLANATION MIGHT BE HELPFUL.

The line started by Senopati, known as the Mataram Dynasty, now consists of two royal lines in Surakarta and two royal lines in Yogyakarta. The Surakarta king is considered a more direct descendant to Senopati and has seniority in terms of ritual, but the Yogyakarta sultan has more practical political influence.

The Queen of the Southern Sea is considered the consort of the monarchs of both Surakarta and Yogyakarta.

The central Java royal line, as with every major royal family in the world, has endured feuds, arranged marriages, power-grabs, and Shakespearean schemes and scandals. The royal families have been manipulated, bribed, and mistreated by Dutch and English colonialists; in turn the royal families have been active in Indonesia's independence movement and post-war nation building.

The city of Surakarta, an hour's flight east of Indonesia's capital Jakarta, is held by many Javanese to be the epicenter of Javanese culture. The town of 500,000 is popularly referred to as Solo; this is the city where Indonesia's President Jokowi was mayor. The Surakarta royal lines include the Susuhunan (King) of the Paku-buwono Kraton (the term *kraton* refers to a royal palace and the power vested therein) and the lesser, but by no means insignificant, principality of Mangkunegaran. The two royal lines seem to constantly be engaged in a soap-opera style spat. The Susuhunan of Surakarta refers to the Queen of the Southern Ocean as Kanjeng Ratu Kidul, thereby attributing to her the status of "queen."

The two royal lines in Yogyakarta are the senior Sultanate of Yogyakarta (the line of Hamengkubuwono) and, like the Surakarta, the less influential principality of Mangkunegaran. The Kraton of Yogyakarta refers to the Mermaid Queen as Nyai Loro Kidul, which reflects a lower status than her equivalent in Surakarta – Nyai Loro Kidul is sometimes considered Kanjeng Ratu Kidul's prime minister. (She has other titles as well; the Javanese relish complexities in their mythological genealogies and, some might say, in their everyday lives.) For the sake of simplicity in this non-academic chapter, let's refer to both the Surakarta and the Yogyakarta versions of the queen as Kanjeng Ratu Kidul – The Queen of the South.

IN THE MID-1980S, I INTERVIEWED SRI SULTAN Hamengku Buwono IX of Yogyakarta about his relationship with Kanjeng Ratu Kidul. The sultan was a key figure in modern Indonesia's history; he played a vital diplomatic role during the Japanese occupation in World War II and helped to lead the fight for independence from the Dutch.

His love story with Ratu Kidul is made public every June 21, when the sultan treks twenty kilometers to the dangerous surf on the slate-gray southern coast of Java. There he offers a full set of women's clothing and his own nail and hair clippings to pay his respects.

In 1984 I was granted an audience. In his souvenir-filled Jakarta office, we talked about politics and the role of culture in enriching society and how magic *krises* can be sent by remote control to kill an enemy. But I wasn't sure how to phrase the single question that was the real purpose of my visit. I tried to pose it in a refined Javanese manner. How was it that a man as pragmatic and cosmopolitan as the sultan – he had been vice president of Indonesia and had also held various ministerial posts – could pay tribute every year to a mermaid queen?

Instead of answering directly, Sri Sultan Hamengku Buwono IX offered me sweet tea and told a story.

"One night during the Dutch occupation of Yogyakarta, I, and others who were living in the palace, heard soldiers moving noisily about, as if wearing armor. It is said they were the soldiers of Ratu Kidul protecting the *kraton*." I pressed him for details. "There was no one in the *kraton* except our family and staff," he said matter-of-factly. "But we all heard the soldiers' drums."

I was more than a little skeptical. With astounding patience he explained how Ratu Kidul changes form between that of an old hag and a beautiful young woman, depending on the cycles of the moon. He gave examples of how Kanjeng Ratu Kidul's timely interventions changed the course of Indonesia's history by giving sage advice to himself and other leaders. The sultan didn't quote Shakespeare, but he might as well have. He gave me the Javanese equivalent of "There are more things in heaven and earth, Horatio/ Than are dreamt of in your philosophy." He concluded: "When I was four years old I was already living with a Dutch family, so my brain is in some ways a Western brain. But many things happen which can't be explained in a logical way."

I must have looked bewildered.

The sultan then told me not to get too caught up in a Cartesian view of the world. "You're asking a Western question, expecting a Western analytical answer," he admonished. "But that's wrong. In my view you either accept it or you don't."

Throughout Java there is magic in the air. Accept it or not. One man's myth-enrobed fantasy is another man's hard-nosed reality. In the rainbow-hued world of shifting Javanese cosmology, reality can be as ethereal as a wisp; like religion, like a miracle, like love, you believe it. Or not.

VISITORS TO JAVA MIGHT LIKE TO SPEND A NIGHT AT the Samudra Beach Hotel at Pelabuhan Ratu (literally "Queen's Harbor") on the south coast of Java, scene of a dramatic appearance of the Mermaid Queen.

The story, as told to me by K.R.T. Hardjonagoro – the regent of the Susuhunan's *kraton* in Surakarta – as we nibbled some of the fried chicken for which Central Java is justly famous, went like this:

In 1966 Sri Sultan Hamengku Buwono IX [of Yogyakarta] attended the opening of the Samudra Beach Hotel on Java's southern coast, which of course is Ratu Kidul's home territory.

In the morning, a few hours before the event, a local *lurah* [village headman] asked for an audience with the sultan. The old man prostrated himself and told the sultan that he had had a dream the previous night in which a lady said she wanted her offerings. She was dressed in green.

The sultan, of course, knew that the old man had seen Ratu Kidul. His Highness thanked the humbled old man but explained that he would not make an offering since he was attending the hotel opening in his civilian capacity as minister of defence, and he wanted to separate the affairs of the state from the mystical duties of the palace.

I was outside, near the pool, when the sultan said goodbye to the well-meaning old man. Shortly after I heard the sound of a locomotive. The noise increased until it sounded like ten locomotives were coming toward the beach-front terrace where we were enjoying the hotel's hospitality. Then a ten-meter-high tidal wave erupted from the sea, which had been calm. It washed away the hotel's buffet table and soaked all the visitors. Some trees were knocked down. Someone ran to tell the sultan what had happened, and realizing what had occurred, the sultan put on his ceremonial clothes, said his prayers to Ratu Kidul, and made the appropriate offerings. The sea was calm once again.

I was incredulous. Hardjonagoro showed me the photos. I said "come on," or something equally un-Javanese. Instead of arguing, he simply told me to go to the hotel and ask for Room 319. Sometime later, I did. This, it turns out, is the room in which Sultan Hamengku Buwono IX made peace with the easily irritated Mermaid Queen. It is kept locked and reserved only for her. For a tip, hotel staff will allow people access to it so they can pray to the Queen of the Southern Ocean. It is a good business.

LIKE OTHER ASIAN MYTHOLOGICAL ICONS – LIKE Ganesha, like the White Elephant, like Kuan Yin – Kanjeng Ratu Kidul is likely a compilation of cultural greatest hits. Historians (who enjoy scrambling for minutiae and esoteric clues in old manuscripts, crumbling temples, and the hidden corners of their own imaginations) have theorized that Kanjeng Ratu Kidul might be related to the Tantric goddess Tara, to an animistic nature spirit, to a universal Earth Mother. Maybe all of the above.

Culturally, the Javanese are a nation of hoarders, hanging on to dusty ideas and legends that just might, you never know, come in handy someday. For example, historian Roy E. Jordaan studied the architecture, inscriptions, and legends of Candi Kalasan, an eighth-century temple that is a short distance from Yogyakarta, and came up with the not-impossible idea that Ratu Kidul evolved from an animistic spirit that evolved into the Hindu mother goddess Uma (or Parvati, or Durga, take your pick), who morphed into the Green Tara of Tantric Buddhism. Like Green Tara, like Uma/Parvati/Durga, Kanjeng Ratu Kidul has a fearsome side and a benevolent side. (Some wags might suggest this indicates she is the ultimate female goddess, unable to make up her mind.) And, like Green Tara, she changes form between an old hag and a beautiful maiden based on the moon's cycle. All the members of this cosmological sorority have a relationship with the sea and with sacred Naga serpents, possess a reputation as protector of navigators, and share a protective fondness for the color green.

But these analyses are rarely clear-cut. We could be making this too complicated.

Kanjeng Ratu Kidul might be something simpler, a nature spirit given human form. In *The Religion of Java*, Clifford Geertz says Ratu Kidul is "perhaps Java's most powerful single *lelembut*," referring to her origin as an ethereal spirit. Or Kanjeng Ratu Kidul might be a marine version, separated by birth perhaps, of her twin Dewi Sri, the Javanese rice goddess who is unremittingly terrestrial.

She could be none of these things. Or all of them. The point is that Javanese accumulate beliefs like a chef cooks a curry. A bit of animistic chili? Of course, throw it in. Some Hindu cardamom, nicely grilled and pounded? Can't hurt. Some Buddhist turmeric, golden and subtle?

Absolutely. Some Islamic prayers and Christian guilt? Sure, the more the yummier.

WHATEVER HER ORIGIN, KANJENG RATU KIDUL CAN be fierce. While her main residence is in the turbulent sea south of Java, she has a terrestrial weekend bungalow in Mount Merapi, one of the most volatile of Java's forty-five active volcanoes. Javanese royal geomancers point out that a powerful energy line runs between the coastal cliffs of Parangtritis on the southern coast, the *kraton* of Yogyakarta, and the summit of Mount Merapi.

Mas Penewu Surakso Hargo, better known as Mbah Maridjan, was the gatekeeper of Mount Merapi appointed by the sultan of Yogyakarta and paid one dollar a month to act as the intermediary between the people and Kanjeng Ratu Kidul. When I visited him in his simple home on the high slopes of the volcano, he greeted me warmly and was gracious with his time, even though a stream of visitors waited patiently for his advice and blessings. He described his job as being "to stop lava from flowing down. Let the volcano breathe, but not cough."

When Merapi erupted in October 2010, Mbah Maridjan refused government orders to evacuate. He was probably killed instantly and his body was found in a praying position.

How can we rationalize the conflicting concept that Kanjeng Ratu Kidul is an oceanic spirit with the belief that she also controls land-based volcanoes? Mbah Maridjan echoed Sri Sultan Hamengkubuwono IX and suggested it's neither unlikely nor impossible for a spirit to have power over water and fire. After all, she appears as a young beautiful woman sometimes and as an old hag other times. This is a classic Asian duality, the dynamic that makes the world continue to spin. Dry season/rainy season. Male/female. Yang/yin. Day and night. Courage and fear. Feast and famine. The evidence for this dualism is visible on every bit of Mount Merapi's slopes – a laboratory of destruction and growth. Like the Hindu god Shiva, Kanjeng Ratu Kidul destroys in order to rebuild. Soon after land has been burned and covered with ash, Kanjeng Ratu Kidul welcomes back farmers with some of the most naturally fertile and productive land in Asia.

She also destroys in order to punish. After the 2010 eruption, my friends explained that Ratu Kidul was angry at her Javanese subjects for abject corruption, the lack of respect for Javanese norms, and abandonment of Javanese culture. Many cultures have a similar end-of-the-world scenario. When things get too dirty, too confused, and too corrupt, it's time for a cleansing and rebirth.

And here's where omen-watchers have a field day. The 2010 eruption destroyed Mbah Maridjan's house and village, but the village mosque was left intact. And a few months after the eruption I toured the golf course of the Merapi Golf and Mountain Resort. The course was in a direct line to be hit by Merapi's lava and ash flows, but only a few holes were slightly damaged.

Sri Sultan Hamengkubuwono X, son of the Indonesian hero I interviewed, is governor of the Special Region of Yogyakarta. The manager of the golf club, Yuandala Kolopaking, told me that the governor plays golf on the Merapi course about once a week. The slopes of Mount Merapi are known for heavy rainfall, but according to Kolopaking, it never rains while the sultan is on the course. Once he gets into his car, however, the heavens open up. Is Kanjeng Ratu Kidul looking after her consort when he plays on her home course?

THE *BEDOYO KETAWANG* WAS ORIGINALLY PERFORMED AS a six-hour marathon, all the better to put the dancers and audience into a trance-like state. Today, the occasional ringing of guests' cell phones reminds us that we live in a faster world, and the dance has been shortened to ninety minutes. Nevertheless, the atmosphere is both picaresque and otherworldly, as the special gamelan orchestra pings and glongs a deliberate beat that accompanies a high-pitched singer, whose voice, to my ears, is screechy, atonal, and melancholy. According to Nancy K. Florida of the University of Michigan, the verses first recount Senopati's setting forth to battle (or to a romantic encounter), then evoke the depth of Kanjeng Ratu Kidul's passion for Senopati and his royal successors, ending with her praise of the metaphysical potency of her lovers.

In the wrong frame of mind, the *bedoyo ketawang* is as tedious as an Andy Warhol movie, but when I remembered my friend's advice to "switch mode," it became a hundred times more entrancing and a thousand times more elegant. Just as western Baroque music has been shown to induce relaxation (and learning) by reducing a person's heart rate and decreasing blood pressure, I have the impression that the *bedoyo ketawang* music, played on sacred gongs and xylophones used only on this occasion, alters our consciousness. Let's call it a Ratu Kidul-enhanced altered state.

The problem is that although we were seated near the front of what might be called the "commoner's section," we had lousy sight lines and had to crane our necks to see past two-meter-tall statues of Greek goddesses and semi-clothed angels, huge Chinese vases, potted ferns, wrought-iron rococo balustrades, and a handful of photographers.

Nevertheless, we saw nine young women wearing dark blue and white batik sarongs, colors that esoterically symbolize earth and ocean, light and darkness. They wore hair extensions pulled back in chignons entwined with golden filigree and jasmine garlands. They had been rehearsing for weeks and were forbidden to dance if they were menstruating.

DURING THE RECEPTION THAT FOLLOWED THE DANCE, a man named Ki Radu Kusumodiningrat approached me and asked if I wanted to "speak with Kanjeng Ratu Kidul." I wasn't too sure what he meant but said yes anyway.

Ki Radu Kusumodiningrat, a relative of the Susuhunan, is a traditional healer. He introduced us to his colleague, who ordinarily works as an acupuncturist and massage therapist but is also a medium. We stopped at a market to buy fruit, candles, and incense and went back to our hotel for the séance. The doorman busted us for the pungent-smelling durian, and out of respect for the no-smoking signs in the room, we canceled the incense, but the medium, Raden Ayu Retno Handayati, wasn't perturbed. She put on her veil and intoned an Islamic blessing. When her voice shifted to the timbre of that of a young woman, we suspended belief and imagined we were speaking with the Mermaid Queen herself.

We asked her about her love affair with Senopati and received romantic platitudes, sort of Javanese Hallmark card sentiments.

"Were you present just now at the *bedoyo ketawang*?"

Raden Ayu Retno Handayati, perhaps channeling Kanjeng Ratu Kidul, smiled and answered enigmatically, "I'm always present for the sultan."

After a few other specific questions and vague answers, we saw she was getting tired. But just before the channeling ended, the queen offered me personal support and invited me on a date, Javanese Mermaid Queen-style. "Just go to the southern coast [of Java], call your name, stamp your foot three times, and I will be there for you."

I wasn't sure what to make of this. Did Raden Ayu Retno Handayati really channel the spirit of the Mermaid Queen? And what kind of reception would I get if I actually went to the beach and sought out Kanjeng Ratu Kidul? Stories are rife about men who wear green

(Kanjeng Ratu Kidul's favorite color) while swimming in the Southern Ocean and are never seen again — perhaps victims of the treacherous riptides, perhaps whisked away to her watery castle.

I AM INTRIGUED BY THE POSSIBILITY THAT KANJENG Ratu Kidul was present at the dance, and I put the question to one of the *bedoyo ketawang* dancers. Wuri, 23, was a soft-spoken English teacher at a local elementary school in Solo and didn't find the question strange. "Yes, I had a feeling Ratu Kidul was there. One time I made a mistake in my hand movement and I felt her correcting me."

Another dancer, Putri, 21, acknowledged that toward the end of the performance she felt a breeze, as if Kanjeng Ratu Kidul was "going to the sultan."

THE MORNING AFTER THE *BEDOYO KETAWANG*, WE RAN into one of the susuhunan's close relatives, who was staying at the same hotel we were. Over croissants we asked the elegantly dressed woman about the previous day's performance and whether she thought Kanjeng Ratu Kidul had appeared.

"Absolutely," she said. Her eyes started to get misty, and a dreamy look, wonderful to see in a woman of a certain age, came over her face. "There was a rush of cool air. That was the queen, going to the king."

Again, I tried to ask a Cartesian question in a polite way. What did she make of all this?

In a wistful voice, perhaps more suited to a love-struck school girl, she answered, "It's a love affair for the ages."

POWER BEYOND JAVA

"Let me show you Ratu Kidul's influence in Bali."

I was with my old friend Anak Agung Gede Rai. He took me to the Inna Grand Bali Beach, a landmark in Sanur, a district in southern Bali known for supernatural encounters and the first upscale resort community on the island. At the time of construction, in 1966, the hotel was a beacon of Indonesia's potentially bright future. It was built with funds provided by Japan as compensation for World War II crimes against the country, along with similarly grand (and similarly designed) hotels in Jakarta (Hotel Indonesia), Yogyakarta (the Ambarrukmo Palace Hotel includes a building that was once a guest house for visitors of an earlier sultan of Yogyakarta), and Pelabuhan Ratu (Samudra Beach Hotel), site of the Ratu Kidul event mentioned earlier.

I knew the hotel well, for this was where I had first met Rai. He was marketing and communications director of the hotel and I handled the hotel's advertising. It was the most imposing building ever built on Bali and will remain so – angry traditionalists said it was too tall and not sufficiently Balinese in spirit; subsequent legislation restricted the height of new buildings to "shorter than the tallest coconut trees." In practice this means a height of three or four stories, depending on the health of your plantation and the height of your ceilings.

Rai told me the story.

In the steamy midday of Wednesday, January 20, 1993, the three-hundred-room Bali Beach Hotel burst into flames with such ferocity that black smoke darkened the sky over Sanur. Huge tongues of flames leapt from the windows of the ten-story building. Almost miraculously, none of the four hundred guests or one thousand staff members were injured.

It was two days before the building had cooled sufficiently for safety officials to enter and assess the damage. They saw that steel railings on the balconies had melted. Guest passports in safe deposit boxes had burned. Every room had been destroyed.

Except for room 327.

Room 327, next to the elevator and staircase, had some smoke damage but otherwise was intact. On the side table, bottles of Aqua drinking water (another client) were undamaged. The bed linen was untouched and complimentary bathrobes hung in the closet. The pictures on the wall dangled peacefully. The plastic telephones, which had completely melted in all the other rooms of the hotel, were undamaged.

Gina Meridiani, the hotel's duty manager who accompanied us to the room, said it was a "miracle" this room was undamaged. The only explanation, she suggested, was that the room had divine protection.

So, how does this relate to Kanjeng Ratu Kidul?

Ah, such a simple question. But answers can be complex.

To understand the involvement of the Mermaid Queen in Bali, one has to understand then-President Sukarno's involvement in Bali.

Sukarno was of mixed Javanese and Balinese descent and so had a pedigree in cultures of the two regions, united through a complex Hindu pedigree.

Sukarno, who died in 1970, took a keen interest in the construction of the large new hotels. Flying over Bali in a helicopter, he identified the spot in Sanur where the Bali Beach Hotel was to be constructed, part of his vision to attract foreign tourists to the at-that-time impoverished country.

Ten days after the fire, Rai asked a senior Balinese priest to perform a cleansing ceremony in the room. The priest, clad in white, went into a trance, Rai said, and saw a man. "Sorry, who are you?" the priest asked. "I'm Sukarno," the spirit answered, and offered three messages related to the fire:

The first comment was, "Don't worry about

the fire; the hotel will be rebuilt soon." And it was. The reconstruction took less than eight months.

Second, the spirit of Sukarno said, "The fire is the fire of revolution. There will be a big change in the country soon. Although not "soon," Indonesia's long-standing President Suharto was forced from office in 1998, five years later, thereby ushering in a major shift to democratic governance.

Third, the Sukarno spirit instructed that room 327 should be kept as it is. "When they heard that comment, the hotel's Board of directors didn't dare to change anything," Rai noted.

I took off my shoes and was allowed into the room. The wallpaper was brown from smoke, but the wooden cupboards and cabinets were undamaged, the twin beds were intact, the vomit-green carpet was unscathed, and the plastic telephone was untouched on the night table. I parted the flimsy curtains and saw a pleasant view of the hotel garden and the sea.

But the offerings of pilgrims had made the space into a cluttered and eclectic shrine. Photos of Sukarno looking confident and smiling his seductive grin. An Indonesian flag. Many pairs of ladies's shoes. Images of Ganesha. An antique kris. Incense and plastic flowers. And, sitting on a shrine, a copy of a famous painting of Kanjeng Ratu Kidul. Javanese hotel staff and guests had decided that Ratu Kidul, a Javanese spirit, was somehow involved in this Balinese miracle.

After some ten minutes, Gina asked us to leave, explaining, "A couple is getting married in the hotel tomorrow and they've come to ask for Ratu Kidul's blessing."

WOMEN ON TOP

In May 2015 Sultan Hamengkubuwono X of Yogyakarta named the eldest of his five daughters, Gusti Kanjeng Ratu Pembayun, 43, as crown princess, giving her the title GKR Mangkubumi Hamemayu Hayuning Bawono Langgeng, which loosely means guardian of the eternal beauty, happiness, and prosperity of the world. The sultan, 69, has no sons.

The act has caused a rift within the royal family. None of the sultan's eleven brothers and half-brothers attended the *sabdaraja* (king's proclamation) ceremony. Family members went on a pilgrimage to the royal cemetery in Imogiri in an effort, according to one of the sultan's half-brothers, "to invoke the family's god and ancestors to change the sultan's mind."

The sultan said, "I don't mind getting scolded or questioned by my brothers. I would only be afraid of getting scolded by God."

The Muslim community also protests the succession plan. Aburrada Fourak, a senior imam of the prominent Gedhe Kauman Mosque, argues that "if the next ruler of the palace was a woman, she could not lead Friday prayers, a responsibility that the sultan has fulfilled throughout his family's reign."

The sultan said his decision was based on God's divine revelation sent through his ancestors. He said his successor had to be willing to have a strong relationship with nature, be someone others would listen to, and must understand his or her true identity and origin.

One possible complication might be what kind of relationship a female sultan would have with Kanjeng Ratu Kidul, a widely revered mystical founder of the Mataram dynasty and the spiritual consort of each of the Yogyakarta sultans. Can two strong women occupy the same palace?

Everyone wants a piece of his soul.

RELIGIONS ON THE WING

The four "religions" of modern life promise benefits
that might take a while to pay off.

MINYAMBOU, WEST PAPUA

hen the fundamentalist Baptist missionaries in this isolated valley in West Papua asked for contributions to build a new church, Zakarias chipped in with the most valuable thing he could find – a bird of paradise.

EARLY PORTUGUESE AND DUTCH SPICE-SEEKERS WERE presented with brightly colored bird skins that had no feet. The locals had simply hacked off the appendages, perhaps deciding that a legless bird was more aesthetically pleasing and therefore worth more in trade. The Europeans, however, deduced that the creatures were legless because they spent their entire lives in the air, using a depression in the female's back as an open-air nest. The Portuguese dubbed them "Passaros de Sol," or Birds of the Sun. The Dutchmen who followed the Portuguese dusted off their Latin vocabulary and named the creature "Avis paradiseus," or Paradise Bird.

THE IRONY OF BUYING HIS WAY INTO HEAVEN WITH A bird that represented holy salvation to the early European conquerors did not occur to Zakarias.

What he did recognize is that proponents of four "religions" want a piece of his soul.

Zakarias showed me chunky grey caterpillars that nature conservationists encourage him to raise. These will become gaudy, yellow and black swallow-tailed butterflies that when sold to collectors will earn him a welcome few dollars each. For a couple of years he had undertaken the extra work strictly as an act of faith – he had received promises of a payback, but no guarantees.

To the conservationists the butterfly venture represents a philosophy that opines that conservation of the rainforest will work only when local people get some tangible benefit from it. The quid pro quo in this case is that Zakarias agrees to help manage and protect the Arfak Mountains Strict Nature Reserve, in the "bird's head" corner of the Indonesian half of the island of New Guinea.

Call it what you will: a new way of saving nature, an example of "sustainable development," an unreliable promise. I call it a religion. In effect, the conservationists have, more or less, convinced Zakarias to change his behavior in return for a possible future reward. "Do not clear land for farms in the nature reserve," the conservation commandments say. "Respect the national park boundaries and enter not therein except to hunt deer with a bow and arrow. And don't even think about killing that bird of paradise."

THE CONSERVATIONISTS ARE AMONG THE MOST BENIGN of the new religionists.

I count at least four *nouvelle* faiths: the belief systems propagated by the government, the churches, the businessmen, and the people who promote nature conservation.

The Javanese who run the country from distant Jakarta want to "Indonesianize" Zakarias by encouraging him to speak Bahasa Indonesia, to follow the civic principles of the national philosophy called *Pancasila*, and to ignore the disruptive Free Papua Movement campaigning for independence.

Fundamentalist Protestant preachers want to "Christianize" him, and by doing so add his tenor voice to the Sunday choir.

Tycoons who manufacture shampoo and jogging shoes want to "consumerise" him, by making him feel the need for things his people have not needed for millennia previously.

And conservationists want to "empower" him, to give him a voice in saving nature, as long as it coincides with the way the Western experts think conservation should work.

"Trust us," these modern-day evangelists seem to say.

"We're from the government/church/business/nature conservation sect. We're here to help you. If you believe in us, even though we give you no guarantee, your life will be improved."

The four "religions" of government, church, business, and conservation have achieved some significant results.

For example, some Christian missionaries in West Papua have helped stop cannibalism and infanticide, have established schools and clinics, and have initiated community development projects like water systems and gardens. But the conversions are not necessarily deep. While many people profess to be Christian, of one form or another, it is not uncommon for Papuans to believe that sitting in church will result in immunity from sickness and that forgetting to shut one's eyes during prayers will lead to blindness.

IT ALSO SEEMS THAT SOME SOCIETIES OUT HERE ARE retrograde cargo cultists at heart.

I was told this, perhaps apocryphal, story. An American missionary had a disciple, a young man he had hoped would go off and undertake God's work in another valley. The missionary and his wife and two kids lived in a prefab house that someone (surely not them) had somehow lugged up into the mountains. Although he had known the Papuan would-be-missionary for several years, the American Bible-thumper had lived aloof from the community and had never invited the acolyte into his house. Finally, the American felt the local lad had passed all the hurdles but one. He suggested the young man join the family for a Coke, whereupon he asked him, "How will you know that you are the best Christian you can be?" The local man, who had grown up in a village without running water or access to medical care, gazed around the inner sanctum, taking in the sight of a television and VCR, a radio-phone, a microwave, a refrigerator, and a boom box, all powered by electricity generated by a tiny hydroelectric system the missionary had asked the local people to construct on the stream behind the village. The young man pondered the question, because it was important for him to get it right. Finally he replied: "When I have all the things you have."

Sounds like the *koreri* cargo cult – a widespread Melanesian belief that if proper rites are performed, the ancestors will bestow good health, food, and material goods – hasn't died out completely, but merely morphed into a slightly different ritual in which the good Hatam people of Minyambou raise their voices to Jesus every Sunday, before depositing a sweet potato in the collection box.

CLEARLY THE SOUL IS A COMPLICATED ORGAN. THE day I was leaving Minyambou, I sought out Zakarias to say goodbye. He admired my watch. Seeing that I wasn't about to give it to him, he offered me a trade: my Casio for a bird of paradise skin. I said a prayer for all of us.

Petrus Bambut, one of the four small people at Kampong Arkel, with one of his daughters.

SEARCHING FOR SMALL FOLK
AT THE END OF THE TRAIL

*A visit with three types of Hobbits
on the isolated Indonesian island of Flores.*

KAMPONG ARKEL, FLORES

*Imaginary short people fascinate us, and they take up an inordinate
amount of space in literature and mythology. We're all familiar with the
Lilliputians who entrapped Gulliver, Snow White's pals Dopey, Sleepy,
Grumpy, and the rest of the Seven Dwarfs, the Munchkins in* The
Wizard of Oz, *the dwarf Mime in Wagner's* Ring Cycle, *Rumpel-
stiltskin, and, of course, Tolkien's Hobbits.*

"top. Over there. See him?"
Our driver, Antonius, had indeed spotted the
tiny man and was already hitting the brakes.

My Indonesian friend Boedhihartono and I hopped
out of the car to introduce ourselves to a middle-aged guy
named Markus, a perfectly friendly, perfectly articulate,
otherwise normal-in-every-way man who happened to
stand no taller than my waist.

Illustrating that Americans have no monopoly on
rudeness, Boedhihartono started grilling the short man

about how he felt to be one meter tall ("OK"), whether his parents were "normal" ("Yes"), if he knew about *Homo floresiensis* ("What's that?").

"Just a midget," Boedhihartono said as we got back in the car and left the village of Kisol.

I checked later and found that about one in forty thousand children worldwide can be defined as a "little person." Uncommon, but not as scarce as the rarities we were seeking.

Most cultures relish their "short folk" stories. The Irish have their leprechauns, the Icelanders their elves, Hawaiians their menehunes, and Scandinavians their tomtar. Worldwide, people have given at least two hundred tongue-caressing appellations to imaginary small folk, with some of the most mellifluous being abatwa, blue men of the minch, bugalademujs, and djinn, not to mention Issun Boshi, jimaninas, naiads, nereids, and nixies, and, lest we forget, pixies, selkies, sluagh, sprites, sylphids, vardogls, weisse frau, wichtlein, yumboes, and zips.

WE HAD TRAVELED TO THE EASTERN INDONESIAN ISLAND of Flores with a simple, albeit esoteric goal – to seek *orang pendek*, the Indonesian name for "short people." These diminutive people are the stuff of legends throughout Southeast Asia, and Flores is a rich hunting ground for small-folk tales.

But tales told around the campfire are no substitute for the real thing, and Flores, a dramatically beautiful volcanic island of 1.4 million people that is two and a half times the size of Bali, is home to three themes of particular interest to *orang pendek* researchers.

The first reason to visit Flores is the discovery in 2003 of a child-sized creature that lived just eighteen thousand years ago (other specimens later discovered lived as recently as twelve thousand years ago). The scientists who described the find declared these to be a new species of the genus *Homo*, and named the group *Homo floresiensis*. They said that these proto-humans, standing less than a meter tall (about the height of a modern three-year-old American child), with heads the size of grapefruits and weighing just twenty-five kilograms, were contemporary with *Homo sapiens* but were not direct ancestors of our species. The investigators dubbed the creatures Hobbit Men.

The second trigger for visiting Flores was to investigate tales of *ebu gogo*, a diminutive human-like short person that inhabits the folk tales, if not the contemporary forests, of contemporary Flores.

The third, and most compelling reason was a statement that Boedhihartono had made a few months earlier, in which he had confidently declared, "there are *real* Hobbits living in a village in Flores." To which the only appropriate response was, "What are you doing in July?"

Orang pendek-*like creatures in Asia are frequently mentioned in folk tales and anthropological literature –* tua yeua *in Thailand,* ye ren *of China,* batutut *of Sabah,* sedapa *of Sumatra,* uyan *of Sarawak, and* nguoi rung *of Vietnam, that in our book* Soul of the Tiger, *Jeff McNeely and I dubbed them* untrahom *(unidentified tropical Asian hominoids), or, more colloquially, "snowmen of the jungle."*

ALL THREE REASONS FOR VISITING FLORES – *HOMO floresiensis, ebu gogo,* and real-life Hobbits – are variations on the idea that unusual small humanoids can be found throughout Asia. Reports of wild tropical *orang pendek* have occurred frequently enough in China, Indochina, Peninsular Malaysia, Borneo, and Sumatra to merit a skeptical inquiry. The *orang pendek* occupy a similar eco-cultural niche in tropical Southeast Asia to the larger Himalayan yeti, which is said to inhabit the high mountains of Nepal and Bhutan.

In one frequently quoted sighting, an Indonesian "short person of the forest" was reported on the island of Sumatra during the 1920s. A Dutch settler named van Herwaarden, who found an *orang pendek* in the deep forest, was quoted by the Belgian naturalist Bernard Heuvelmans:

> The very dark hair on its head fell almost to the waist ... [its] brown face was almost hairless. The eyes were very lively, and like human eyes. The nose was broad with fairly large nostrils, but in no way clumsy. Its lips were quite ordinary. Its canines showed clearly from time to time, they were more developed than a man's. I was able to see its right ear which was exactly like a little human ear.

Some respected scientists give cautious credence to the possibility that *orang pendek* might exist. John MacKinnon, the only scientist to have studied the three great apes in the wild, told me that he found footprints in Sabah, Malaysia, of an unidentified primate that were "so like a man's yet definitely not a man's that my skin crept and I felt a strange desire to return home."

Philosopher-scientists have long speculated on man's relationship with apes and "wild men." Pliny elevated apes to "wild men," and Leonardo da Vinci noted similarities between people and animals. Goethe discovered the intermaxillary bone in man and "trembled with delight" about the links this indicated between man and ape. Darwin, fearful of the fallout from creationists, including his devoutly Christian wife, at first avoided the subject of whether man evolved from apes.

Human-like apes roam the territory of primal myth. Most of us sophisticated city-dwellers have separated ourselves from these remnants of the collective unconscious. But I've always been curious about what survival benefits myths and legends have for mankind as a whole.

Among Asia's forest people, who are in daily contact with "wild nature," the various forms of ape-men are an ever-present reminder of what it means to be man-like, yet not quite human. The creatures of the twilight world live in the forest, away from people, and people fear and respect both them and their forest home.

Even far from the rainforest, most societies tell tales of ape-men, perhaps because we need to be reminded of what our life might be like if we did not have culture, that uniquely human attribute. As the British writer Angus Hall suggests: "We need creatures like these to inhabit that strange borderland between fact and fantasy, and our interest lies not so much in whether they really exist but in the possibility that they *may* exist."

Whether they exist or not, *orang pendek* inhabit an arena of research called cryptozoology – creatures in the wrong place or time such as the Loch Ness monster in Scotland, the *Ninki-nanka*, a giant swamp-dwelling reptile reported from the Gambia, and a dinosaur in central Africa called *Mokele-mbembe*, whose name means "One that stops the flow of rivers."

The jury is still out on whether the bones identified as Homo floresiensis *represent a new species. Mike Morwood, an Australian scientist who was part of the research team that excavated the Flores site and published the first scientific papers on* Homo floresiensis, *was convinced, based on the jaw structure, lack of chin, brain capacity, height, relative length of arms and legs, and other details, that they found a new species. Some scientists, notably Indonesia's Teuku Jacob of Gadjah Mada University, suggested that the individuals found were* Homo sapiens *suffering from microcephaly, a developmental disorder that causes the head and brain to be much smaller than average. Subsequently, another theory was proposed that the individuals were* Homo sapiens *born without a functioning thyroid due to an iron deficiency in pregnancy, a developmental disorder known as cretinism, which led to severe dwarfism and reduced brain size. And in 2014, researchers writing in the* Proceedings of the National Academy of Sciences *suggested that the individual from Liang Bua identified as LB1 (Flo) was not a new species but a small modern human who suffered Down syndrome.*

THE MOST IMPORTANT PREHISTORIC ARCHEOLOGICAL site in Indonesia today is Liang Bua ("cold cave"), where *Homo floresiensis* was discovered. The cave lies fourteen kilometers north of the Flores town of Ruteng. Motor-cycles or trucks can cover the last three-kilometer section of bad road. We chose to walk.

Boedhihartono and I visited when excavations had been suspended, in part due to a lack of funding, in part due to inter-agency feuding about which Indonesian government department had the right to explore the cave, and the archeological digs had been back-filled with dirt to deter unauthorized digging. Hendrikus Bandar, the "key keeper" of the cave, showed us around.

The cave itself is in the form of a fat crescent, maybe fifty meters across, with several levels and elevated niches, opening to a green valley where perhaps long ago a river flowed. It was almost too perfect; I could see the site being used as the setting for a caveman movie.

In *A New Human,* by Mike Morwood and Penny van Oosterzee, the authors write that as Morwood was leaving Indonesia after a session of ten weeks of excavation in 2003, he jokingly asked Emanuel Wahyu Saptomo when he was going to find them a pre-modern hominid skull to go with the bones of pygmy elephants, giant rats, and stone artifacts that had been excavated.

His friends obliged and Rokus Due Awe, a sixty-four-year-old paleoanthropologist from Flores, describes the eureka moment when they realized they were dealing with something special. Digging at a depth of some six meters, Pak Benny, one of the researchers, found a "whitish expression in the clay," according to Rokus. In his zeal to see more, Benny accidentally sliced off what turned out to be the left brow ridge of the skull of the first *Homo floresiensis* discovered.

Benny fortunately stopped his trowel work and called Emanuel Wahyu Saptomo to have a look. Wahyu himself wasn't sure what they had discovered and asked Rokus to have a look.

"It's a skull," Rokus said.

"Monkey or human?" Wahyu asked the older man.

"Human," Rokus answered.

"Really? Are you one hundred percent sure?"

"Two hundred percent."

The skull was very soft, "the consistency of wet blotting paper," according to Rokus. They cut around it and took the block of stone back to the Hotel Sindha.

Room nineteen of the Hotel Sindha in Ruteng hardly looks like the control center for a mega-scientific discovery. It's spacious enough, at about sixteen square meters, and the price is right – just ten dollars a night. The room comes with a plain wooden desk, two twin beds with worn floral linen, cream-colored painted cement walls, a mirror, and a pair of electrical wires hanging from the ceiling. In the bathroom the bright yellow sink has stains that defy analysis. There's no hot water, but the friendly staff will boil up a bucket that you can mix with the cold to take a bath, which is welcome since Ruteng is at an altitude of eleven hundred meters and it can get a bit fresh at night.

Before they could study the fossil, the Ruteng crew had to harden the bone, which they did by buying acetone in the local drugstore and mixing it with epoxy glue. The piece of the skull, of a female who was later named Flo, took three days to dry.

Rokus explains those exciting early days:

> First I thought it was from a child about ten years old, but after cleaning it we could see that the teeth were very worn, indicating an age of perhaps 28–30 [equivalent to an age today of 50–60].

The team had just made one of the most sensational discoveries in the history of human evolution.

Rokus Due Awe, a scientist involved in the discovery and identification of Homo floresiensis, *remembers that his father warned his children not to leave the house when it was raining, lest they be captured by an* orang pendek-*type creature called* kuraci *or* ebu ngiu. *Rokus, a Flores native who grew up near Bajawa, explained that the children were told the animal ran very fast, was hairy over its entire body, lived in the jungle, stole vegetables from farms, and was smaller than one meter tall. I asked Rokus, a smiling middle-aged man, whether he really believed the stories. "Yes," he replied, he did. But, perhaps realizing that he had a persona as a scientist to portray, he added, "of course we can't prove anything unless we catch one."*

———————————

PEOPLE IN THIS PART OF FLORES TELL STORIES ABOUT a local bogeyman. Rokus described it as *kuraci* or *ebu ngiu;* most people refer to it as *ebu gogo.* One of its functions is to frighten children. Children should beware of strangers. They should not wander alone into the forest. And, more philosophically, they should reject their "dark" side.

Most cultures have such prohibition-creating goblins; one of the possible origins for the English phrase "bogey-man" derives from stories about Indonesian Bugis pirates from south Sulawesi that British parents living in Asia told their children to get them to behave.

Ground zero for *ebu gogo* is the region around Ebu Lobo ("all ancestors") volcano, at 2,149 meters a prominent landmark. And the main storyteller about *ebu gogo*, which roughly means "ancestor who eats anything," is Pak Epe, the Kampong Boawae headman who describes a creature with a hairy body that lives in caves and eats raw meat and climbs vertical rock faces like a lizard. Boedhihartono and I were skeptical. "It's true," he said. "A female *ebu gogo* has breasts so long that she can flip them over her shoulders."

Epe tells a campfire legend he has down pat. He's clearly told it numerous times before, and he is particularly keen to show us a business card of a producer of the American TV show 60 Minutes who had interviewed him several years earlier.

Epe estimates he's about sixty-nine. He's bald on top, with white flyaway hair on the sides. He has sparkling eyes and speaks in clear Indonesian.

His story, which he claims is "thousands of years old," is simple and fuzzy. Once upon a time, a group of *ebu gogo* came into a village to steal vegetables from the gardens. For reasons that were not clear, one time they stole a five-year-old boy, who was raised by the *ebu gogo*. Years later, they sent the wild child back to the village to steal fire (shades of Prometheus), and he was caught. The villagers forced the boy to show them the cave where the *ebu gogo* lived and the humans proceeded to set fires that killed all but two of the wild men, who escaped to do something, somewhere.

Boedhihartono and I agreed that, as origin legends go, this was pretty feeble stuff. No mythical elements, nothing mystical or sacred, just an old wives' tale that would probably sound better when told around a campfire with the rice wine flowing. As we leave, Epe requests a gift for his time.

We give him a few dollars and ask one last question. "Do the *ebu gogo* still exist?"

"Probably not," he reluctantly decides.

There are many conditions and diseases that can cause short stature, according to Little People of America, a nonprofit organization that provides support and information to people of short stature and their families. The most frequently diagnosed cause of short stature is achondroplasia, a genetic condition that results in disproportionately short arms and legs; the average height of adults with achondroplasia is 1.52 meters. The website dwarfism.org says that this condition occurs in all races and with equal frequency in males and females; there are some two hundred thousand little people worldwide.

TRAVELING WITH BOEDHIHARTONO IS A BIT LIKE spending time with a full university faculty. Although his business card explains that he's in the University of Indonesia Faculty of Social and Political Sciences with a focus on tourism, his Ph.D. from the Sorbonne in Paris is in human ecology, and his Berkeley post-doc studies were in paleoanthropology.

And he's a medical doctor.

He is a man of many quests, of many journeys. One morning Boedhihartono becomes a geology professor, explaining the difference between volcanic felsic and mafic lava flows, then he segues into a few words of praise about James Lovelock's "Gaia Hypothesis," explaining why it's bad to drink cold liquids in hot weather, and weaving in tales of his visits with the remote, magical, and notably xenophobic Baduy people of West Java.

During tea he explains the history of craniometry, and the difference between dolichocephalic, brachycephalic, and mesocephalic skull types.

And after dinner he might take the role of a politically incorrect history of religions professor, urging the Javanese to return to the glory days of the Hindu Majapahit Empire, stressing that Asians should follow Asian religions.

And it doesn't take much to get him to discourse on one of his favorite topics – cryptozoology. Boedhihartono thinks that relict tigers still live in Java (specifically not in east Java where they were thought to have most recently gone extinct, but in west Java) and seeks funding for an expedition. Similarly, and more relevant for our Flores trip, he has been searching for *orang pendek* on the large Indonesian islands of Java, Sulawesi, and Sumatra and on the smaller island of Bangka.

In our modern world, many vertically challenged men and women have achieved greatness. Some examples of short men who have made it big:

> *Sammy Davis Jr., Mahatma Gandhi, Nikita Khrushchev, and Voltaire were short men, standing 160 cm, which is a couple of centimeters taller than Balzac, Buckminster Fuller, Yuri Gagarin, Paul Simon, St. Francis of Assisi, and John Keats, who were in turn relatively tall compared to Henri de Toulouse-Lautrec (150 cm) and the even more diminutive Alexander Pope (137 cm).*

Local people are proud of Liang Bua, and government tourism officials in the regional capital Ruteng are hoping that the *Homo floresiensis*, nicknamed "Flo," will do for western Flores what Brigitte Bardot did for St. Tropez. The Ruteng visitor center has published leaflets and posters showing a rather fanciful drawing of "Flo," and there are plans to pave the dirt road leading to the cave. There are also plans to construct a visitors center near the cave, but, according to Ardi Suardi, an economics professor at Komodo University in Ruteng, the local villagers who own this land are asking about $10,000 for land that might be worth a fraction of that amount, and negotiations continue.

After wandering around Liang Bua we visited neighboring Kampong Rampasasa, just a ten-minute walk, to ask what they knew about *orang pendek*.

We were greeted warmly, as is the case in most Indonesian villages, and escorted into the headman's house, a large airless room with packed earth floor, half the size of a tennis court, which doubles as the community meeting hall. The headman asked if we would like a welcome ceremony, which came in two sizes: the Traditional Lite for five dollars, and Traditional with Rice Wine for ten dollars. I remembered Boedhihartono's warning in Jakarta to "be careful what you eat or drink in the villages." In the safety of Jakarta I had asked what he meant, and he vaguely alluded to the possibility of magic and spells.

But I happen to think that spells only work if the spellee believes they work, and figuring we would get better answers for the extra five dollars, or at the very least contribute a bit to the local economy, we sat and drank, surrounded by the usual assortment of children, old women, and tired men who hadn't gone to the farms that day.

We were asked to introduce ourselves, and Boedhihartono did the honors. The headman translated the potted bios from Indonesian into the local Manggarai dialect, and I whispered to Boedhihartono.

"Boedhi, you're giving yourself all the credit. I'm a university professor too, not just a Western tourist."

I said this, of course, to enhance our dual stature and to show that we were serious men of science and not shallow day-tripping thrill-seekers.

So Boedhihartono reintroduced me, and in spite of the glowing words, which made me sound like the inventor of the Internet, author of more books than Erle Stanley Gardner, and educator of malleable minds the world over, I noticed a wizened old lady look at me with what seemed to be amused skepticism. She murmured, to no one in particular, the universal aspersion used to describe uninvited, inappropriately attired visitors with more money than tact: *"Turis."*

Regardless, Boedhihartono still had me trumped. He was a medical doctor, and after a few swigs of rice wine poured from a large white plastic jerry can, he was swarmed with villagers telling them about their ailments.

And then we asked the requisite questions about *orang pendek*. Have they heard any stories? Are they themselves descendants of the folks in Liang Bua? Are any small folks still alive?

And our ten dollars paid off, or at least confirmed free information we had received earlier. "Not here, but there are some short people up in Kampong Arkel."

And so we set off up the hill.

But what about really short people? Gul Mohammed, the world's shortest man, died in 1997 at the age of forty. He was 57 cm tall, and weighed 17 kg. By comparison, Verne Troyer, the actor who played Mini-Me in the Austin Powers movies, stood at a statuesque 81 cm, and Charles Becker (the actor who played the mayor of Munchkinland in The Wizard of Oz*) towered at just over one meter. By comparison, the Mbuti Pygmies of central Africa generally stand tall at around 150 cm.*

SETTING OFF UP THE HILL IS A COMMON EXPERIENCE in Indonesia when searching for strange happenstances. In Sumatra, near Kerinci-Seblat National Park, I was looking for tiger magicians who could capture man-eating tigers by singing them lullabies.

When I asked educated people living in the large cities of Java and Sumatra about these *pawang harimau*, the answer was usually, "we've heard about these things but that's the domain of our wild, savage, near-naked cousins who live in the snake-infested jungles. Why do you want to go there anyway? No Starbucks in the jungle."

This is the common arrogance of the lowland elite, seen throughout Southeast Asia. Without saying it, people imply, "We're educated, we have a big powerful religion, our culture is active but refined through centuries of subtle evolution, we have good personal hygiene, electricity (TV!), wear attractive clothes, and speak several languages, and we don't want to know anything about what our rural forefathers were doing just a few generations ago."

So I set out to seek tiger magicians, just as I've set out to seek men in west Java who can turn themselves into thieving pigs, and a tribe of giant white cannibals in Halmahera. Each time I get to the provincial capital, I ask around and people roughly point in the direction of the mountains. "Set off into the hills," they say. I'll take a bus, then a motorcycle, then walk to reach the mountains where the villages become simpler, where there are fewer purchased goods, where there might not be electricity or plumbing, and the people will say, "It's not us boss, you want those crazy dudes across the valley and high up the next ridge. Be careful, they've got magic." So I keep on climbing up the increasingly narrow trail, and at the end of the line, far from the nearest road or Internet café, and *really* out of cell phone range, I reach a small village and find people who are quite normal. They have families, they hunt, they might poach a few endangered species, they farm, they respect whatever spirits they think are important, they laugh, they cry. And once in a while, if I ask the right questions in the right way, and if I'm smart enough to figure out "what did that guy really say?", I get some insights.

In a sense, the "over-the-next-hill" attitude reflects the existence of orang pendek stories. By common understanding, people on the coast are handsome, smart, and sophisticated. People in the outback are hillbillies. When you're at the bottom of the social totem pole, how do you maintain your humanity? We define ourselves partly by what we are not. And these end-of-the-line folks have no other social groups to look down on so they create an intermediate creature, more than ape but less than human. These stories consolidate the value and integrity of rural folk, as well as helping to maintain some social control.

FROM KAMPONG RAMPASASA AND LIANG BUA WE walked half an hour and then hitched a ride on a passenger truck to Kampong Arkel, which sits at the top of a steep hill.

Arkel is a small, poor village, without the impressive carvings, statuary, weaving, and visible cultural richness found in some other Flores communities. It has no school. No running water. The end of the line.

In small villages like Arkel, the arrival of any strangers is reason to gather and gawk. The "Hobbits" were waiting for us, almost on cue.

We were quickly introduced to four small people, none of whom was taller than 130 cm. They were the living Hobbits we had sought, the holy grail of our search. It was all too easy.

Four members of the clan's short family were on hand to greet us: Margaretha Ndindis, Petrus Bambut, Yohanes

Jerahi, and Laurensius Jema. Other family members were living in different parts of Indonesia, they explained.

Petrus, the patriarch, said he might be one hundred years old. Boedhihartono was in his element and asked him what he did during the "Japanese war," referring to World War II. Petrus said that when the war started, he had just gotten married but had not yet had children, which would make him about twenty in 1940, and about eighty-five today. Not one hundred as he claimed, but a significant age in any case.

Laurensius Jema is *kepala adat* of the village, the keeper of the traditions. He's married to a woman of normal height and has four children; his brother Yohanes has five.

Their aunt, Margaretha Ndindis, was also of an advanced age, and she asked Boedhihartono for medicine to treat a chronic headache. Boedhihartono obliged, giving her an injection of analgesic on her bum, watched by curious villagers. He was generous with his free medical advice, which reflected his own personal beliefs – eat lots of pork and drink tea without sugar.

While Margaretha was lying on the mat, Boedhihartono got out his calipers and measured the width and breadth of her skull, her nose length, and the width of her mandible and jaw, as he had earlier with Laurensius, Yohanes, and Petrus. The exercise had the feeling of a vet measuring tranquilized critters.

It was getting late and we had to decide whether to leave immediately in order to return to Ruteng that night or stay.

I was prepared to stay – I had some energy bars, my hammock, and a nearly full water bottle, and I argued that we had come all this way and that these were the only Hobbits we were ever going to meet in our lifetime so what's the rush.

But for reasons that were logical but ultimately unsatisfying, we left Arkel late that afternoon. Boedhihartono argued that the village people were poor and would be embarrassed because they couldn't feed us; there was no water, no toilet. And he speculated that they were getting bored by us, and we had already asked all our questions and wouldn't get any more information. The unspoken subtext was that Boedhihartono was tired and had a cough and wanted to sleep in a bed in town.

On the walk down I asked Boedhihartono whether they were Hobbits based on their cranial measurements. "Well, they're short people," he answered, a touch too enigmatically.

Mike Morwood thinks that Homo floresiensis *might have been in existence as recently as two thousand years ago, which would easily put it into the cultural memory of any people who had an unbroken presence in the region since then.*

THE BAY AT LABUAN BAJO, ON THE FAR WESTERN corner of Flores, is one of the more scenic in Indonesia, dotted with islands and rock outcroppings. Local businessmen have built dozens of inelegant restaurants and guest houses along the main drag to provide accommodation to thousands of tourists who use Labuan Bajo as a starting point for a visit to Komodo National Park, which lies to the west, home of the famous dragons and world-class scuba diving.

Emanuel Wahyu Saptomo, of the Indonesian archeological service, and his colleagues were staying at the Hotel Bajo, convenient, but hardly romantic or luxurious – they had no view of the harbor and the bamboo-walled rooms did little to stop the *vroom* of motorcycles zapping past every few minutes.

Wahyu was cautiously excited. The headman of Rangko village, on the north coast of Flores, had visited them telling of an exciting discovery. Two young men had found a human skull in a cave. The headman was no doubt hoping that this was an anthropological discovery that would rank alongside the Liang Bua dig, and would therefore bring fame and a bit of fortune to their small coastal community of seven hundred fishermen.

We quizzed Wahyu about the possible importance of the discovery, but the discussion broke down into furtive whispering every few minutes while Wahyu periodically excused himself to make phone calls. Later he explained that he hadn't been sure about whether I, having the odd double distinction of being a journalist and a foreigner, could go with them to the village the next day, but his superiors gave him the go ahead with the request that if it turned out to be a big discovery, I wouldn't write about it until after scientific tests had been completed.

The next morning we took a *bemo* to a neighboring village and boarded a boat for a pleasant half-hour trip along the northern coast to Kampong Rangko.

We climbed an hour up a steep hill to Goa Intan, "Diamond Cave," so-called because when the walls are wet the silica in the stone reflects sunlight like jewels. The cave had graffiti scratched on the wall, in English: "wel/com to/gua intan."

And the discovery? We found shards of earthenware pottery, shards of green-glazed pottery, which Rokos identified as Yuan Dynasty, bones from a large rodent, some remnant human humerus bones, and the *pièce de résistance*, a large chunk of a human skull, which had been previously excavated by villagers.

It took Wahyu about thirty seconds to burst the headman's bubble. The skull was indeed human, perhaps six hundred years old, and distinctly not of significant evolutionary value. But, being Indonesian and inherently polite, Wahyu promised to discuss the matter with his colleagues and report back to the eager villagers. I don't know whether they were too poor or too disheartened, but the fishing folk in the village didn't offer us lunch.

ON OUR LAST DAY IN FLORES, AN EVEN MORE INTRI-guing story emerged, again originating from the isolated northern coast of the island.

Hearing of our interest in strange creatures, we met a gentleman named Pak Nico, who said that in his isolated coastal village one night he heard a screeching cry. It "sounded like something out of that dinosaur movie," he said, referring to *Jurassic Park*, which apparently had made its way to the TV broadcasts of this distant corner of Indonesia. He did not see anything, but his fellow villagers swore they had viewed a frightening T-Rex-like creature that climbed trees and ate pigs and goats. It's called *marengket* in the local Mangarai language, Pak Nico said. Boedhihartono and I were still skeptical, since tales of *orang pendek* and their ilk are frequent, but until you capture one all you have is a good dinner-party story. But Pak Nico added that several years ago, a villager had killed one of the animals but had neglected to keep the bones. Imagine, a relict dinosaur that lives on the north coast of Flores. And I know where it is – a long day's journey in a four-wheel drive vehicle, then a couple of hours walk. Not far at all.

The spice at the heart of colonial exploration.

Photo: Jon Connell

THE LAST PERKENIER

How could one now-ignored spice have generated such mayhem?

BANDA, MOLUCCAS

 sought out the last *perkenier* of Banda.

In 1992, when I took a tiny boat from the main island of Banda Naira to the adjacent island of Banda Besar, I found Wilhelm "Benny" van den Broecke sitting on his porch, as if he had been expecting me.

In Benny's living room hung a copy of a famous and valuable painting of Benny's ancestor, Pieter van den Broecke, who came to Banda with Jan Pieterszoon Coen in the early seventeenth century and became the Dutch East India Company (VOC-Vereenigde Oost-Indische Compagnie) administrator in the Banda islands. The 1663 painting by Frans Hals shows a prosperous, smiling, large-nosed burgher with untidy hair, long moustache, and pointed and waxed "van Dyke" beard, wearing a brown velvet shirt decorated with lace on the wrists and collar. He has the look of a mischievous man-about-town.

Benny, by comparison, was a sixty-something, skinny, unglamorous man of mixed ancestry (his mother was Indonesian, father mixed Indonesian-Dutch). On his aging skinny legs he wore thin brown socks and faded blue scuba diving booties. He remembered better times.

I soon learned that in order to understand Benny I had to understand his ancestor Pieter van den Broecke, who lived fourteen generations earlier. And that meant understanding nutmeg, a now-insignificant commodity that changed the world.

NUTMEG WAS KNOWN IN EUROPE FOR SOME TWO thousand years, supplied by Chinese, Malay, and Arab traders who traded small quantities of the spice.

In the first century A.D., Roman historian Pliny wrote of a tree bearing nuts with two flavors. In the sixth century, nutmegs were brought by Arab merchants to Constantinople, and twelfth-century Holy Roman Emperor Henry VI had the streets of Rome fumigated with nutmegs before his coronation.

Nutmeg, *Myristica fragrans*, has been used in Western medicine since at least the seventh century. During the Elizabethan period, frightened lords and ladies in England sought nutmeg as a cure for the plague. More mundanely, it was widely used as a flavoring, general medicinal tonic, and preserving agent. In the nineteenth century it was used as an abortifacient, which led to numerous recorded cases of nutmeg poisoning. It's difficult to us today to grasp the importance and perceived value of nutmeg since it has now been relegated to the status of a novelty spice, used sparingly by Americans to flavor eggnog and pumpkin pie.

But in its heyday, nutmeg (along with cloves from Ternate) was the holy grail of merchants and conquerors.

Nutmeg had all the attributes of a precious commodity – it was scarce and therefore ridiculously expensive. It came from a distant land whose location was a closely guarded secret. To obtain the spice, a merchant (or country) had two choices – pay an exorbitant amount for delivery at home, a price involving a cut to a dizzying number of profit-seeking traders. Or send out navies and merchantmen and administrators to largely uncharted and dangerous waters to try to find, and then to manage, and finally to control, the source of the fruit. This was a high-risk/high-reward pastime.

And, to make the nutmeg story even more tantalizing, it came from just one tiny island group in the back-of-beyond, the island group we now call Banda.

Rarely has such a speck of real estate had such a major impact on global history.

UNHAPPY WITH HAVING TO PAY DOZENS OF MIDDLE-men for their nutmeg, Portuguese, Spanish, British, and Dutch mercenaries and navies searched for, and finally visited, the Spice Islands to establish their own line of supply. The quest for the origin of exotic spices, and more specifically the desire to *control* the spice trade, led to a period of dramatic global exploration and generated mayhem and bloodshed on a cinematic scale.

FOR THE SAKE OF THIS TALE LET'S JUMP TO THE DUTCH period.

A HUNDRED YEARS BEFORE PIETER VAN DEN BROECKE arrived, in the early sixteenth century, Italian traveler Lodovico de Varthema found the Banda islands "savage" and the people "like beasts ... so stupid that if they wished to do evil they would not know how to accomplish it." This disdain for the people of Banda made its way to Holland (Jan Pieterszoon Coen wrote "[the Bandanese] are indolent people of whom little good can be expected. [They] should be overpowered, the chiefs exterminated and chased away, and the land repopulated."

For their part, the Bandanese had an equally low opinion of the Dutch. In his book *Nathaniel's Nutmeg*, Giles Milton quotes a declaration from the elders of Banda that "all of us ... do utterly hate the very sight of theis Hollanders, sonnes of Whores, because they exceede in lying and villainy and desire to overcome all men's country by trechery." (The eloquence of this statement suggests that it might have been ghostwritten for the

Bandanese by the Dutch-hating English of the time, but that could be simply my cynicism at work.)

A fight was inevitable, and it was neither fair nor pretty.

IN 1621 DUTCH SOLDIERS LANDED ON BANDA NAIRA ISLAND.

The Bandanese *orang kaya* (literally "rich men" who were the local authorities) were forced at gunpoint by the Dutch to sign an unfeasibly arduous treaty, one that was in fact impossible to keep, thus providing Coen an excuse to use superior Dutch force against the recalcitrant Bandanese. The Dutch quickly noted a number of alleged violations of the new treaty, in response to which Coen launched a punitive massacre. Japanese mercenaries were hired to deal with the *orang kaya*, forty-four of whom were decapitated with their heads impaled and displayed on bamboo spears. (We think of globalization as a recent phenomenon, but as far back as the 1600s much of the world, at least the coastal areas, was known, mapped, and visited; hence Jan Pieterszoon Coen's employment of some eighty Japanese samurai – whose compatriots were also employed by various kings and sultans throughout Southeast Asia – to subdue Banda.)

In addition, it is suggested that perhaps fourteen thousand people on Banda, out of an estimated total population of fifteen thousand, were killed by Dutch muskets and Japanese swords, making the seizure of Banda one of the most brutal corporate takeovers in history. The

Dutch subsequently resettled the islands' nutmeg plantations with imported slaves, convicts, and indentured laborers. The VOC directors in Amsterdam later concluded that Coen should have acted with greater moderation, but nevertheless awarded him a bonus of three thousand guilders for his commercially valuable services.

Thus began, initially under the flag of commerce and later under direct government rule, more than three hundred years of Dutch colonial control of the Spice Islands.

WHILE THE DUTCH WERE BULLYING THEIR WAY TO authority in Banda and neighboring islands, the British were also trading in the islands and negotiating treaties with local rulers, much to the consternation of the Dutch.

The result: fierce battles, Byzantine intrigue, and unholy alliances. And excessive inter-European brutality: early seventeenth-century Dutchmen imprisoned their English counterparts under the Dutch latrines, torturing them with a form of water-boarding and blowing off bits of their limbs with gunpowder bandages. In one two-decade period, some one hundred fifty Englishmen were murdered by the Dutch and another eight hundred were sold into slavery.

THE MERCANTILE WORLD BUILT ON ECONOMIC MONO-
polies run by government-supported trading companies
was evolving into a system of direct control by foreign
governments – what we term the colonial period. The
VOC was formally dissolved in 1800 and its colonial
possessions in the Indonesian archipelago were nation-
alized under the Dutch Republic as the Dutch East Indies.
In 1858 the British government took direct control of
India from the British East India Company, and in 1863
France conquered southern Vietnam.

TWO OF THE MOST IMPORTANT DIPLOMATIC TREATIES
of the early colonial period were the 1494 Treaty of
Tordesillas (which split the world into a half "owned" by
Spain, and a half "owned" by Portugal), and the 1667
Treaty of Breda, a complicated pact involving England, the
United Provinces (Netherlands), France, and Denmark.
As part of this treaty, which did not name the islands in
question, England, which had control over the tiny Banda-
controlled island of Run but little else in the region,
traded Run to the Netherlands in exchange for the Dutch
territories in the New World. One of the Dutch territories
in New Netherland (a region rich in beaver pelts that
includes the current mid-Atlantic states), was New
Amsterdam, later known as Manhattan.

THE ISLAND OF RUN WOULD FIT COMFORTABLY INTO Manhattan's Central Park.

THE ENGLISH MIGHT HAVE LOST CONTROL OF THE Spice Islands, but they didn't go quietly into that dark night.

During the years of seventeenth-century skirmishing with the Dutch, the English, being skilled horticulturalists as well as clever businessmen, liberated a bunch of nutmeg trees from Banda and transplanted them to their own colonial holdings elsewhere, initially Ceylon, Malaya, and Singapore. (This botanical piracy was a very British form of colonial economic warfare – in 1876 the British sabotaged the Portuguese monopoly on rubber when Henry Wickham stole seventy thousand wild rubber seeds from Amazonian Brazil. The seeds were planted in London's Kew Gardens. Only twenty-eight hundred germinated but that was enough – the resulting domestic seedlings were sent to British colonies in Ceylon and Malaya where they thrived, thereby all but destroying Portuguese overseas influence and wealth.)

Another blow to Dutch hegemony of the nutmeg trade occurred from 1769 to 1770 when French horticulturalist and administrator Pierre Poivre (what an appropriate name for a spice smuggler), stole seeds of nutmeg and other spices from the Indies for replanting in Mauritius and the Seychelles.

Nevertheless, although their monopoly had been chipped away, the Dutch continued to hold control of the Spice Islands until World War II.

FLASHBACK TO 1621.

Pieter van den Broecke came to Banda in that year with Jan Pieterszoon Coen, and was appointed administrator of the region.

Pieter van den Broecke's life was as colorful as his portrait. Early in his career, while in Mocha, Yemen, he drank what he described as "something hot and black, a coffee." He was one of the first Europeans to describe societies in West and Central Africa and to develop trade strategies for commerce along the African coast. After capturing a Portuguese ship in 1611, he transported a cargo of some thirty thousand kilograms (sixty-five thousand pounds) of ivory to Amsterdam (if the thirty thousand kilogram number is accurate, this represents some twenty-five hundred African elephants).

After decimating Banda's population, Jan Pieterszoon Coen divided the productive land (on which grew some half a million nutmeg trees) into sixty-eight smaller estates. These land parcels were then handed to Dutch planters. With few Bandanese left to work them, slaves were brought in; the VOC paid the *perkeniers* just 1/122 of the Dutch market price for nutmeg. Nevertheless, the *perkeniers* (although widely used in Dutch, Indonesian, and English history books and articles, the Dutch term *perkenier* rarely appears in dictionaries of those languages. It is roughly equivalent to the English term "planter" or "estate manager" but is only used in the context of nutmeg and other spices grown by Dutchmen in eastern Indonesia) still profited immensely and built substantial villas with opulent imported European decorations, such as the once-glamorous but now rundown 1718 villa in which Benny lived.

I ASKED BENNY TO SHOW ME THE FRUIT THAT CAUSED such a fuss.

He handed me an apricot-sized capsule. On breaking the brown fibrous outer shell, I saw a bright red filigree with the consistency of glossy electrical tape surrounding a shiny black nut. The filigree, which resembles a bicycle helmet, is the mace; the nut is the nutmeg.

The mace is stripped off and left to dry in the sun.

The nutmeg is roasted for a week on the second floor of a heating shed near Benny's house, producing a sweet and musky incense-like smell.

IN THE HEYDAY OF NUTMEG PRODUCTION IN PRE-independence Indonesia, Benny's family had a one hundred-hectare (247-acre) plantation, but after independence in 1947, the Indonesian government "stole" much of it leaving Benny with only twelve hectares and a few thousand trees. To add insult to injury, Benny notes that the price of nutmeg and mace has crashed because Indonesia doesn't support independent farmers like him. The quality of nutmeg and mace from Grenada is better than that grown in Banda, he says.

"In 1958 there were thirty-four *perkeniers*," Benny says. "Now it's only me."

DES ALWI, OFTEN DESCRIBED AS THE UNOFFICIAL KING of Banda, whom I knew since the 1970s and who died in 2010, was a larger-than-life character, a nonstop raconteur, and a tireless promoter of his home.

He was also an Indonesian freedom fighter rebelling against Dutch rule.

It's possible that Alwi would not have become an Indonesian revolutionary hero except for a quirk of history that has the satisfying ring of cosmic justice.

As a young boy growing up in isolated Banda, Alwi was taken under the wing by two prominent Indonesian rebels who had been exiled by the Dutch to Banda to keep them out of politics. Mohammad Hatta, who after independence became the first vice president of Indonesia, and Indonesian intellectual Sutan Sjahrir, who became the country's first prime minister, saw promise in the young and outgoing Alwi and helped foster in him a gift for diplomacy, self-confidence, and a thirst for independence that stood him in good stead later in life.

The few times I had met Alwi, it was early in my time

in Indonesia and I didn't know the right questions. If I could visit with him now, I would ask, "Do you think all this fuss and bloodshed was worth it just to control a few pungent spices?"

I WANTED TO CLIMB GUNUNG API VOLCANO (LITERALLY "mountain of fire"), which sits on its own island just across the harbor from Banda Naira.

Gunung Api isn't terribly high, just 667 meters (2,188 feet), but the ascent takes a hot, tiring two and a half hours through scrub and over scree.

From the summit of the volcano I got a better idea of the tiny archipelago's appeal. Adored by scuba divers, revered by history buffs, appreciated by photographers, and cherished by romantics, the Banda islands are/were on the radar of visitors such as Mick Jagger and the late Princess Diana and Jacques Cousteau.

As I rested on the edge of the summit, two things in particular stood out.

The first was the sight of Run island in the distance. A tiny, isolated speck of land that, as they say about a great boxer, fought above its weight. I later took a small boat to Run just to be able to say I went there. I visited a small village, where people were friendly but didn't talk much about the island's place in history. They were blissfully unaware that Run had been traded for Manhattan. I wanted to go for a swim and a stroll around the beach. My boatman was in a hurry to return to Banda Naira. "Storm's coming," he mumbled. "And anyway there's not much here."

The second memory was the presence of the volcano itself, which last erupted in 1988.

Volcanoes are the Asian epitome of dynamic opposites – male/female, yang/yin, sun/moon, day/night, dry season/rainy season, exploration/nurturing, and the ultimate set of antagonists: good/evil. Volcanoes kill, but then life returns in even greater fecundity. They are solid but fluid, inspiring but destructive. They create chaos, but inspire poets. They are fickle, an appropriate place for the gods to call home. They incinerate farms and chastise people for ill deeds, yet after an eruption all forms of life, including people, return to the volcanoes, for they are the home of the plants and animals and people as much as they are the home of the spirits.

AFTER CLIMBING THE VOLCANO I TOOK A STROLL INTO the village of Banda Naira. I was tired, sweaty, in search of a cold drink. A young girl, maybe ten years old, smiled at me, probably with pity that a foreigner would come all the way to Banda to exhaust himself climbing a volcano, and offered a greeting I hadn't heard before in Indonesia, "Hello, Friend."

Don't mess around with dragon logic.

Photo: Jones/Shimlock-Secret Sea Visions

DRAGON'S BREATH

It's not a good idea to get too close to a Komodo dragon.

KOMODO NATIONAL PARK

In one of the best examples of bad judgment since General Custer declared, "let's head out to Little Big Horn and teach those renegade Sioux a lesson they'll never forget," Sharon Stone's husband, Phil Bronstein, was induced to enter the Los Angeles Zoo cage of a rare Komodo dragon.

The zookeeper had told Bronstein to take off his shoes – the cautious zookeeper, using zookeeper logic, thought that the dragon might mistake Bronstein's white running shoes for big white rats. The quick moving dragon, using reptile logic, instead chomped on Bronstein's big white toe, sending him to the hospital for major surgery.

Bronstein is executive editor of the *San Francisco Chronicle*, and some of his opponents reacted with rather vicious schadenfreude. A Bay Area political consultant suggested that a trust fund be established for the dragon, which he speculated had suffered food poisoning. San

Francisco Mayor Willie Brown, oft-criticized in *Chronicle* editorials, said "I wish the person who suggested Mr. Bronstein remove his shoes had advised him to go in naked."

Although I have never had the pleasure of marrying Sharon Stone, my life parallels Bronstein's in one sense – I too have had a run-in with a Komodo dragon.

My encounters with Komodo dragons took place in the wild. The animals are found only in Indonesia's Komodo National Park and parts of neighboring western Flores, some five hundred kilometers east of Bali; approximately twenty-five hundred dragons remain.

Although park officials have stopped the practice of hanging recently slaughtered goats at a dried riverbed to provide easy viewing of the reptilian carnivores, Komodo dragons are still easy to spot.

We saw our first dragon, a juvenile about a meter long, soon after we alighted at the national park's dock.

A few steps later we encountered a bunch of adults – lazy, nasty-looking brutes that can reach a length and weight similar to that of an NBA center – lounging around the staff quarters of the national park station, attracted to the smells of lunch being cooked. "Don't get too close," Abdurrahman, the park ranger, said. "They look slow but they can move quickly."

KOMODO IS A WORLD HERITAGE SITE, FAMOUS NOT only for its dragons but also for its coral reefs, which are among the most exuberant in the world. The day before our dragon encounter, we had gaped at fish and coral that took on the undisciplined colors of a child's paint box. There was little subtlety here, just nature designed by God during her Salvador Dalí phase. We saw meter-tall vertically ridged barrel sponges, pink-gray and resembling ancient amphora, with technicolor-feathered crinoids on the sponges' edges, waving in the current like tiny underwater prayer flags. We admired hard and soft corals, sea snakes, and turtles. Even the names evoked exotic extravagance: damselfish and anemones, clownfish and fire urchins, zebra crabs, nudibranches and fan corals.

Diver and writer Kal Muller described an Indonesian coral reef as a "time machine, ten million years out of synch with land, a reminder of the time when all the life on Earth existed in shallow tropical seas, soup of creation." Corals first appeared on earth some 240 million years ago, roughly about the same time as the ancestors of Komodo dragons. I had come to Komodo from Bali and was reminded of the Hindu mythology of that wondrous land – the Earth was formed when the Naga, the cosmic dragon, churned the sea of milk.

ON THE NARROW TRAIL WE CREPT UP ON A FEMALE dragon. We were already too close for safety, about two meters away.

The dragon was a female, and she was guarding a mound of leaves and detritus behind her that indicated a nest full of dragon eggs.

"Can we look at the nests?" we whispered, pointing to the clumps of leaves that lay in a protected cul-de-sac behind the dragon.

"Okay, but don't startle her," Abdurrahman cautioned. We left the half-meter-wide path and scrambled, not too daintily, around the half-sleeping dragon. At one point we were merely a meter away. In hindsight, this was a Bronsteinian-scale stupid idea.

The dragon flicked her forked tongue at us as we clambered past, one of the Komodo dragon's several snake-like characteristics. Abdurrahman stood guard with a flimsy stick, ostensibly so that we wouldn't learn more about her other snake-like attribute – the ability to disjoint her lower and upper jaws in order to swallow large chunks of prey. The dragon's prehistoric prey were pygmy elephants called stegedon that were as short as a child; today the dragon thrives on deer and goats and doesn't even have to disable its dinner. Even a slight nip will work – the animal's toxic and septic saliva will kill a wounded animal within hours, and all the dragon has to do is follow the trail of its rapidly weakening prey.

We examined the mounds of dirt and leaves, nests abandoned by ground-dwelling megapode birds in which dragons lay their three dozen eggs. The decomposing compost provides the heat to incubate the dragon eggs, but the female has to keep guard to ward off other predatory and cannibalistic dragons.

THIS WAS FASCINATING, BUT THE REALITY WAS THAT WE were in a cul-de-sac and had no choice but to retreat past the female dragon in order to resume our trek. Finally, gingerly, we shuffled past her. While she seemed more intent on her nap than lunch, I was reminded of the Swiss baron, Rudolf von Reding Biberegg, who, during a visit to Komodo in 1974, fell and injured his knee. His guide ran to a village to seek help. All the search party found was the man's hat, camera, and a bloodstained shoe. Von Reding, 79, a seasoned hunter, made the ultimate contribution to nature conservation – he fed himself to an endangered species.

Climb the mountain and the Dragon Princess might jump-start your new career.

Photo: Jones/Shimlock — Secret Sea Visions

WANT A BUSINESS BOOST? MAKE FRIENDS WITH THE DRAGON PRINCESS

Komodo dragons, woodcarvers,
and the princess who controls them all.

KOMODO VILLAGE, KOMODO NATIONAL PARK

I t never hurts a wannabe businessman to have the support of the Dragon Princess.

Aside from several high-powered local busi-nessmen who allegedly made their fortunes selling illegally obtained reef fish to Chinese middlemen, Ishaka Mansur is far and away the most prominent businessman in Komodo National Park.

Ishaka, 54, carves wooden sculptures of Komodo dragons, the world's largest lizard, which is only found in this area, a one-hour flight east of Bali.

I found his house easily – his name is in the tourist guidebooks and Komodo village is a tiny place. He has enough business to sustain a workshop of ten carvers, who whittle under his tutelage much like the assembly-line studios of the great Renaissance painters. His statues sell for fifteen dollars for a dragon not much bigger than my hand, up to more than two hundred and fifty dollars for a full-size two-meter replica. That's good money in a region where poor fishermen are lucky to break into the cash economy at all.

And Ishaka owes it all to a special woman.

Like many romantic mysteries, the tale began on a tropical beach at night.

"It was in November, 1982, at the beginning of the rainy season," Ishaka remembers. "I was alone and suddenly saw a beautiful woman come down from the mountains behind the village."

Ishaka's wife sits nearby and listens, with no obvious reaction. Undoubtedly, she's heard it before.

Wearing a T-shirt emblazoned with the phrase "Dragon Princess" and a green-checked sarong, Ishaka continues.

"This beautiful woman – much prettier than any movie star, suddenly said, 'Marry me.'" Ishaka glanced over at his wife. "I told her, 'I have a wife.'"

"She isn't as strong as me," the beautiful stranger replied.

Suddenly, Ishaka remembers, his pressure lamp went out. The beach became dark.

"I'm original Komodo," the strange woman said, switching from the national language of Bahasa Indonesia into an archaic form of the local dialect.

According to Ishaka, she urged him to go with her to her home in the mountains, but he refused, not wanting to worry his family by not returning to the village.

Nevertheless, they made a date for the following night. Ishaka was to come alone and follow the river to the top of the mountain. She gave him an egg-shaped gray rock to show him the way.

"When I returned home that first night, my wife was angry," Ishaka says. "She didn't believe my story. Then I took off my shirt and had *naga*, dragon, markings all over my neck and chest."

Ishaka explains this while sitting in his village home, decorated with a few old Dutch plates, a poster of Muslim prayers, and photos pasted on the wall showing him with the American ambassador, taken during a cultural exhibition in the distant Indonesian capital of Jakarta. A small crowd has pushed into his home to gawk at me and perhaps sell me some pearls. Outside, under a shade tree, Ishaka's carvers continue a gentle chatter and soft chiseling while they turn logs into souvenirs.

Ishaka explains that when he reached the summit, a large stone suddenly turned into a palace. Then the woman appeared. "She told me to call her *Ratu Puteri*, Princess," Ishaka says. "She wore a fine silk sari, like an Indian, but she was a Komodo woman."

"It was strange and scary and I pleaded with her not to kill me," Ishaka recalls.

Instead, the Dragon Princess caused a door to open and Ishaka was ushered into a huge room with a table laden with all sorts of delicacies. "We sat on cushions on the floor while we ate. She explained that if I had a problem, I should make an offering and she would appear to me as a *naga*," he explained, referring to the Hindu dragon based on the king cobra. "She said that if anyone in the village killed a dragon, they would become crazy."

Then came the vocational advice.

"You must leave your job and start carving dragons," she instructed him.

And the rest, as they say, is history.

I examine his carvings. His statues are even sold in the United States through the assistance of The Nature Conservancy, which tries to develop income-generating activities in Komodo as a means to promote nature conservation.

I compliment him on the fluid nature of his sculptures, which are quite sophisticated compared to the clunky efforts of other Komodo carvers.

"All my wooden dragons are alive," Ishaka explains. "They have the Dragon Princess's essence."

WHAT DOES THE FUTURE HOLD FOR KOMODO'S HUMAN POPULATION?

While Ishaka's business model prospers, things are less secure for other Komodo residents.

For a start there is the small but real threat of

an attack by a Komodo dragon. Since the national park's establishment in 1980, dragons have killed two people and maimed others. There is discussion about building fences to separate the reptiles from the people.

Then there's basic quality of life. On these poor, arid islands the Indonesian government, assisted by The Nature Conservancy and other conservation groups, has built five new schools, dug wells for fresh drinking water, and established a free mobile doctor service.

And finally, there's economics. The villages in and around the national park have doubled in size over the past decade, which means it is harder for some people to make a living. Efforts have been made to stop destructive dynamite fishing; villagers can engage in low-impact fishing in designated areas. Income-generating projects help people produce souvenirs for sale to tourists, cultivate seaweed, and breed high-value reef fish (such as grouper and wrasse) as an alternative to fishing threatened wild fish populations.

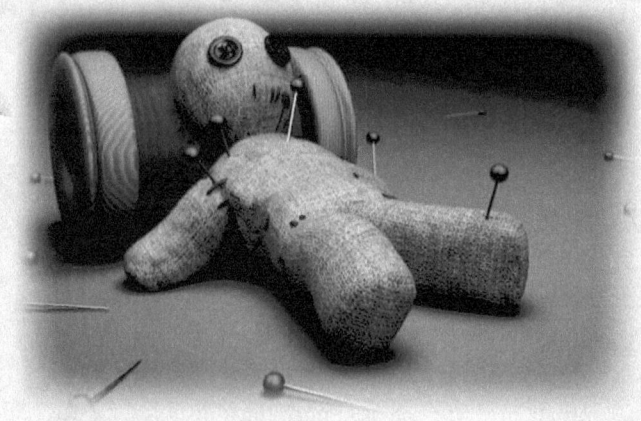

The dark arts burn brightly.

THE MAN WITH PINS
IN HIS LUNGS

*After dinner in Sulawesi, chatting with a man
who has a message from Moses.*

BOGANI NANI WARTABONE
NATIONAL PARK, SULAWESI

ver the grilled fish I ask about spirits.
We are eating lunch in a simple *warung* outside
Bogani Nani Wartabone National Park in north
Sulawesi. I sense that my companions have tales to tell.

Endie is the daughter of a senior official in the
Indonesian customs service. Suddenly her father fell ill,
she explains, and for three years he passed blood in his
urine. The eerie thing was that this only happened when
he was in Indonesia. When he went for treatment in
Singapore, Taiwan, and Belgium his urine was normal, but
once he returned to Indonesia the blood returned. The
doctors were baffled. One day, when it was clear he was
dying, her father's assistant came to the house and

announced, "My mother, who is a *dukun* [shaman or medium] told me to come."

The younger man confessed that he wanted Endie's father's job, and to get it he had put a spell on the older man, the materials for which included the boss's picture, a small *kris*, some rice husks, palm fibers, needles, and a shroud. By way of explaining his strange admission he added, "My mother says I must confess that I put a spell on you in order to cleanse my soul."

The young man came from Aceh, a land in north Sumatra some three time zones to the west, a region with a reputation for strong magic, which made it easier for Endie's family to understand his behavior.

Endie and her siblings asked her father whether they should take revenge. "No," he answered. "God will decide his fate." Her father died three days later. The murderer, if such he may be called, got the coveted job but was arrested four months later for corruption.

I ask Endie what she makes of all this. "I used to not believe in this mumbo-jumbo," she says. "I do now."

She asks me what I make of it. "If I believed that the man actually did put a spell on my father, then I would have taken revenge. That's the Western approach. An eye for an eye and all that."

Endie shakes her head. "No. Let it be. The account will even out by itself."

ONE FINDS MAGIC THROUGHOUT INDONESIA, INDEED throughout Asia, but Sulawesi, shaped like a malnourished orchid and the world's eleventh largest island, has a particularly powerful reputation as a place where strange things happen.

The Protestant part of north Sulawesi, called Minahasa, is famed for its dining options – spicy dog, grilled bat – charbroiled wild animals of all description can be found in the smaller village restaurants of the region. However, we were in the southern, predominantly Muslim region of north Sulawesi where the diet is more generically Indonesian. We ate curried chicken with our fingers and traded ghost stories.

We talked about how Manado is famed for black magic, and someone joked that Yuli, one of the women in our group, a woman who knows how to make herself attractive to men, resorted to black magic to snare her current husband, a much older senior government official who happened to also be present at the table. The understanding was that trophy-wife Yuli snagged her husband by putting a powerful spell on her paramour. Such "love-magic" is commonly used, or at least commonly accepted as real, by many Indonesians throughout the archipelago. There was some nervous laughter, but Yuli and her husband took it well and didn't deny it.

We turned to Yan Mokoginta, a member of Parliament, and he told us a startling story that no one questioned. Yan's daughter is a physician. She had a patient who complained of chest pains and coughs, and an X-ray showed that the patient's lungs were filled with needles, a common mystical condition that is often cited when people trade stories about voodoo-like spells. Yan's daughter told the man that there was nothing she and her Western medicine could do for him and suggested he see a *dukun*. The man with needles in his lungs went for a *dukun* treatment and returned a few weeks later, feeling just fine. The second X-ray showed nothing in his lungs. The needles had disappeared.

As we approached the car, Yan Mokoginta took me aside. "Come to my family's house. There is someone you should meet."

YAN MOKOGINTA'S FAMILY HAS LARGE LANDHOLDINGS in this part of northern Sulawesi, but his brother's house was simple, Indonesian middle-class. Stone floor, white-washed walls. Plastic flowers. Brown upholstered furniture. A muted red and grey leaf pattern on the curtains over the doorways. Two paintings hung on a far wall – fish and reindeer – in dull colors.

We are four – Yan, a family friend named Sukardi, and Yan's brother, Usman Mokoginta, who has a long face like a seal's, with slicked-back hair. Casually, almost off-handedly, Usman tells me he sees two *other* men in the room. I see nothing, but Usman assures me that he sees two other visitors – a big man with a long white beard and long white hair who wears a white wool cap, jacket, and tie; and a second man, also tall, wearing a black jacket and tie, bald. Usman asks if this second man could be my father, who died years ago. "No," I answer. "My father was short and had all his hair."

"Then he must be a *jaga*," he decides. Guardian. Bodyguard.

I HAVE BEEN TO SEE NUMEROUS FORTUNE TELLERS and mystics, prophets, and holy men. Usually I feel neutral in their presence. I am curious but not a believer. I wait to hear what they have to say. I am cynical; I am strong. Like the song, I am a rock.

Although Usman gave me a wrong guess about my father's physical stature, tonight I find myself apprehensive. My posture is twisted. I try to center myself; my body remains off balance. I taste my lunch.

I am sitting with my back to the doorway. I sense someone at the entrance, and I turn around just in time to see a man poke his head in the front door then withdraw it. In that instant I feel frightened, partly because of his unusual entrance and immediate exit, but more because of what I see. The man, whose name I learn later is Mansur, has a generous moustache, wavy black hair, and a mischievous smile. After a moment he enters the room and we shake hands. He reminds me of a man I have never met – my Pavarotti-resembling grandfather, whom I know only from a single photo.

"*Makan dulu*," Yan says. Let's eat first. We enjoy a robust, dog-free meal and then retreat into a smaller room, a bedroom. Through the thin walls we hear the soundtrack of the TV in the next room – an international tennis match is being played in distant Jakarta, several thousand kilometers away; Carl Uwe Steeb is beating Michael Chang.

The room is hot and crowded. We sit on the floor. My back hurts and I lean against a bed post.

Mansur – the man who reminds me of my never-met grandfather – sits cross-legged. He bends forward, puts his right hand to his forehead, then thrusts out his hand. At that moment Sukardi, who is the medium, suddenly shivers, pounds his chest, hits his forehead with a fist, shakes the fist, and makes an abrupt rowing motion. He hunches his shoulders, and his posture resembles that of a bear. His hands shake. He points to a spot next to me. "Your father. He's there. Small body." I look at Sukardi's eyes. Previously normal, his eyes now protrude like those of an ornamental goldfish, inbred for generations to create grotesque bubble-like eyes.

"Your father is very clever, likes to write," Yan says, trying to translate. But Yan has trouble following, since Sukardi speaks partly in an archaic form of Bahasa Mongondow, the local dialect.

Sukardi hunches again and lurches, a stylized movement that reminds me of Javanese *wayang wong*, where men dance like wooden puppets. He reaches to shake each of our hands.

"You've made contact with your father three times," he says. This is true if you count that I had visited three other mediums who claim to have made contact with him.

I ask if my father is all right. I am instantly annoyed with myself for posing such a mundane and ridiculous question.

Sukardi speaks with a gruff, theatrical voice. Mixed in with the words are guttural, animal-like sounds. A growl, a cough. "He's a writer, like you."

No, I think. *You're wrong. He's not a writer like me. He's a dreamer, like me.*

I ask about a man called David, without explaining that he is my son.

"He is smart. Do whatever you feel is right. Your father will help."

"What will happen to my son?"

"He will be like you."

Sukardi has been giving me vague answers and I am full yet unsatisfied, the Chinese dinner syndrome in a spiritual context. I reflect on the strange circumstances that brought me here. I had met Yan Mokoginta in Jakarta more than a year earlier, through Russ Betts, head of WWF in Indonesia. I was interested in Yan's work in developing the Alfred Russel Wallace University in the Bogani Nani Wartabone National Park. Since then we had lost contact. Then, in an example of traveler's seren-dipity, I ran into Yan at the Makassar airport in south Sulawesi.

The circumstances were curious, as if a benign cosmic intelligence was at work. I had planned to fly on a Sunday from Denpasar to Manado, and then go by road down to Bogani Nani Wartabone National Park. My flight had to transit in Makassar. A friend convinced me to leave on the Monday instead. Turns out that Yan was on a Monday flight from Jakarta to Makassar, which connected to my flight. His destination? Manado and then Bogani Nani Wartabone National Park. He was traveling with Gunawan Satari, the number two man in the Ministry of Research and Technology, and officials of the Indonesian Red Cross, the British Council, and the Wallacea Development Institute. They were preparing a workshop on biodiversity in the Wallacea region. They invited me to join them for the recce and to come back for the workshop several weeks later. Coincidence? Destiny?

"Your son is in Java," Sukardi says, taking a guess.

"Yes."

"Jakarta."

Not really. He is in Bogor, forty-five minutes from Jakarta. Close enough.

And then he tells me something about my family that shakes my smug Western cool.

I sit stunned. This man has no way of knowing what he just told me. He has no business in knowing that. I stare at the man with Marty Feldman-like bulbous eyes, legs folded, shoulders hunched like a Neanderthal, speaking an ancient language. He's been giving me softball answers and then comes out and tells me something I have told few people. Is he reading my mind or does he have deeper powers? The medium grunts. My spine feels like a pretzel.

I need to change the subject, but instead of asking a happier question, I persist with something potentially ominous. "What about *jodoh*?" What is my fate?

"You have two destinies. Romance and work. You have success in both, but need great patience."

Predictable softball answers. "My mother?"

"Sick." He makes asthmatic sounds, massages his leg.

I explain she's dead.

Sukardi extends his hand, and, acting as medium, conveys my parents' love to me.

Most of the medium's comments have been vague, generic, inconclusive, and unconvincing. But he was right about my family secret, and Mansur uncannily resembles my grandfather. Logically, there is nothing to this, but I am strangely, uncomfortably distraught. Sukardi and I are both shaking. "Your parents protect you."

Sukardi closes his eyes and shudders. His body relaxes and he "awakes." He does not remember the previous half hour and asks what happened.

Later I ask Mansur how he got his gift. He explains he has only had it for two years, since he was forty. He had had a dream in which he was fighting against many people when the force came to him and he was able to vanquish his enemies. Now, whenever he is in trouble, he listens to a voice that tells him what to do.

BEFORE WE LEAVE, YAN MOKOGINTA, THE POLITICIAN and landholder, disappears with his brother into another room. I assume they are talking about family matters. Back in the car, however, Yan tells me what his brother said.

"Remember the man my brother saw protecting you at the beginning of the evening? The big man in white?"

I remember.

"That was Moses. Moses protects you."

I don't know what to make of that. I don't want to hurt Yan's feelings, but I also have trouble taking this too seriously. Again, someone (or something) gives me the wisdom to shut up.

"My brother also saw Moses protecting *me*," Yan says. "We both have a task. You are Jewish. I am Muslim."

"And what is the task?" I ask.

"Peace in the Middle East."

"Yan, I can't get away. I have a book to write," I protest, trying to lighten the mood.

"Not now. You don't have to go now. The time will come," Yan says. "But that was Moses."

THINGS THAT GO BUMP
IN THE NIGHT

I'd wager a big bet that virtually every Indonesian has had a close encounter with a spirit, ghost, or unexplained phenomenon – either personally or through the experiences of a relative or friend.

Lumped together, conveniently if not always accurately, such spiritualism defies black and white categorization. Lee Khoon Choy, a former Singapore ambassador to Indonesia and author of *Indonesia Between Myth and Reality*, said:

> in Indonesia, myth and reality are sometimes so blurred that even Indonesians themselves find it difficult to draw a dividing line between the two.

As Sultan Hamengkubuwono X of Yogyakarta told me, believe such things, or not. But don't question mysterious things too closely, nor examine them with just a Western eye. The shadow world loses its definition when the light is turned up too brightly or dimmed to darkness.

My Javanese friend Bantan, a senior diplomat with the United Nations and a graduate of prestigous universities in the United States and Canada, often tells me about strange occurrences he and his family have experienced. I prod and ask whether he really believes in such things.

"No, I don't," he says. "I don't believe in spirits or ghosts or *djins*. But these things happened. I can't explain them; I don't know what to believe."

My host, Pak Pisondodo.
Not quite the giant white cannibal I was looking for.

IN SEARCH OF THE LOST
WHITE TRIBE OF HALMAHERA

Where have all the giant Caucasian cannibals gone?

TOTODAKU, HALMAHERA

 suspected a search for a lost tribe of giant white cannibals in eastern Indonesia was going to be a touch problematic.

In 1993 my eyes widened as my friend Albertus Paspalangi, a fisherman who lives on the tiny island of Bobale off the New Jersey-sized island of Halmahera, told me about a tribe of very tall, very naked, and very xenophobic cannibals who kill unwanted visitors by hurling stones with their feet and eating their victims raw.

Paspalangi, who has spent his entire life on the coast, said the Orang Togutil live in the isolated hills on the far side of this K-shaped island in eastern Indonesia.

I decided to look for these curious people, although my experience told me that the odds of actually finding such ethnic oddities are only slightly better than locating Brigadoon.

FOR TEN YEARS I HAD WANTED TO VISIT THE ORANG Togutil (literally "Togutil People") in Halmahera, some three time zones and thousands of kilometers from Indonesia's capital Jakarta, but info was scanty.

With the help of friends who work for BirdLife International, which is hoping to establish Halmahera's first national park in the deep forests occupied by the three thousand or so Togutils, my friend Bill and I ventured into the far end of this seldom-visited island.

It wasn't all that hard actually. Starting from the volcano-dominated island of Ternate (historically famous as the origin of cloves and base camp of Alfred Russel Wallace, who developed the theory of natural selection while in Ternate), we took a few journeys in open boats to reach the depressing dusty frontier town of Subayim on Halmahera. We then climbed on the back of motorcycles for a dusty hour, then walked for another forty-five minutes.

We came to a small village of twenty-five families, and the Togutils were sitting around, as if waiting for us. Right away it was clear that this wasn't the wild lost white tribe.

ALBERTUS PASPALANGI, MY FISHERMAN FRIEND, IS A "lowlander." Although he certainly isn't rich, he has a nice house, he follows a monotheistic religion, he speaks the national language, he sends his kids to school, he has electricity and a TV, and he knows the names of

Indonesian politicians and pop stars. He's never been to the interior forests of Halmahera and has no interest in doing so. To him, the interior is a place of jungle and potential danger. Given the chance for a holiday, there's no question he'd head for a city like Jakarta and not to inner-Halmahera.

He's not at all an evil man, but he perpetuates a "we" vs. "them" attitude that has been at the root of "brown-brown" discrimination existing since city/states were created. The same dynamic is at work in regard to destruction of nature – my American ancestors "conquered" the West by decimating Indians and wildlife; today's American leaders propose to drill for oil and "conquer" the Arctic Wildlife Refuge in Alaska for the benefit of people in the cities. And throughout the tropics, governments and entrepreneurs feel little remorse in "conquering" the wilderness – whether that wilderness consists of forest-dwelling people or tropical forests.

EVERYONE, REGARDLESS OF HOW LOW THEY ARE ON THE social totem pole, needs to be superior to some other group. But what happens when you live at the end of the trail? How do you define your place in human society?

PHYSICALLY, THE TOGUTILS LOOKED SIMILAR TO OTHER Indonesian hill tribes, although considerably poorer and less sophisticated. They certainly had a simple life – few people in their tiny community spoke Indonesian, they didn't grow rice, they hunted for deer and wild pigs with simple bows and arrows. A couple of the older men wore loincloths but most wore shorts and T-shirts. The Togutil weren't totally out of the mainstream – Christian missionaries had built a small chapel in the village.

More dramatically, the Togutils were neither white nor tall nor nasty. They seemed quite happy for us to spend a few days with them.

BILL AND I WENT FOR A WALK WITH ONE OF THE OLDER Togutil, Pak Pisondodo, curious to see how he hunted with just a handmade bow and arrow.

Pisondoldo was born in 1957 but looked ancient – short and skinny with a wispy beard, wearing a loose loincloth made of faded and torn batik held in place by a strip of rattan, his wide calloused feet never encumbered by shoes.

We heard the distinctive whoosh of a pair of Blyth's hornbills in flight, one of the many protected birds in these forests. They were safe from Pisondodo's simple bamboo arrows, which are accurate only at short range because they have no fletching to guide them in flight.

We tried to tread softly, but of course no deer or wild pig in its right mind would hang around when it heard clumsy Europeans stumbling through the forest. Realizing there was little need to keep quiet, I asked Pisondodo about the legends that his people were tall, white, and fierce.

"Oh, that's not us," he said. "You want the Orang Lingon. But be careful. Those guys are mean. Very *galak*. Fierce. Eyes like sharks. Powerful magic. They eat people raw."

My informant on Bobale had clearly sent me to the wrong isolated tribe.

Pisondodo explained that the Lingon made themselves hard to find, living in the deep forest without fixed settlements.

Would he be willing to take us to look for them?

Pisondodo shook his head no. "Those Lingon are *really* savage."

DO WE NEED NATURE OR FEAR IT?

We seem undecided about our relationship with nature.

On the soft, fuzzy side, we need nature. We come from nature, we are part of nature. Nature feeds us, physically and emotionally. This connection is very ancient, very Jungian in its impact on our collective unconscious. Our earliest ancestors – well before the development of agriculture and writing, before the wheel and fire – groveled with other animals, fought them for carrion, found shelter in the forests, opportunity in the plains. They understood, at least unconsciously, the cycles of rain and drought. Our ancestors came from nature; nature was part of them. This may explain why today the presence of green scenery slows our blood pressure and relieves stress. It might explain why people working in bleak, anonymous offices nurture houseplants to brighten things up, and why people recover faster from surgery when their hospital window has a view of a park (curiously, even having a photograph of nature speeds healing compared to a barren wall). We have what could be termed a female/yin approach to nature – we are part of the global scheme of things, the interwoven tapestry of life – mysterious, complex, sharing, questioning, supportive, fertile.

But what about the fear? We define ourselves partly by what we are not. We are no longer "savages" who coexist with animals; we are civilized, we have left the darkness. Our ancestors learned to use plants for medicine, build complex shelters, and after much trial and error, to dominate nature by mastering fire, making metal tools, growing crops, and domesticating other animals. We became the masters of the universe. We have civilization, language, plows, and guns. In the Christian sense we possess "dominion" over nature as opposed to, say, the Buddhist or Traditional Beliefs approach of living in "harmony" with nature. We are male/yang: logical, goal-driven, suspicious of outsiders, confident, potent. Conquerors. That's why we're uncomfortable when "undisciplined" nature approaches too close. We tend our manicured gardens and engage in a Sisyphean battle against dandelions in order to "manage" nature. That's why most first- and second-generation urban people in Asia will look at you askance when you explain that you're going into the deep forests. You're likely to get a response like, "Ugh, full of snakes!" or "No cell phone coverage" or "Go to the shopping mall instead." It's all a way of saying, "the forest is alien, it's dangerous, it's filled with people having strange animistic beliefs who worship spirits that reside in the trees and streams and volcanoes." Perhaps the heart of our fear is that we're afraid of looking too deeply into the mirror and seeing our savage side.

We're part of nature yet we want to dissociate ourselves from anything too wild. Where do you stand?

Who's in control here?

WE BETTER COLLECT THE BIRD NESTS BEFORE THE OUTSIDERS GET HERE

In isolated eastern Indonesia, the tough question is who owns the resources.

JIRLAI, ARU

hat could be more exciting than being with men who walk into the forest wearing faded basketball shorts, encumbered only with hand-made bow and arrows, accompanied by only a couple of dogs, and return home an hour or two later with a deer? Where in the world are people still so independent and self-sufficient?

With my friend Mark van der Wal, and a small team of researchers and support crew, I met two local men – Ely and Yos – in the tiny village of Jirlai on the island of Aru, just off the western coast of the much larger island of New Guinea.

I asked Ely and Yos how they made money. They explained they sell birds of paradise, edible bird's nests made from the saliva of swiftlets, and deer jerky. Had they lived on the coast of this rarely visited island, their answer likely would have been sea turtles, sea cucumbers, mother of pearl, and sharks' fins. They rely on nature, and one of their main sources of cash – the birds of paradise – are protected species.

Even in as isolated a place as Aru (a Puerto Rico-sized island some four time zones and five flights from the capital of Jakarta) people need some cash – to pay school fees, to buy kerosene and monosodium glutamate and beer and soap, to buy a T-shirt and a going-to-church dress for the wife.

How ironic. We envy them for their simplicity. They envy us for our possessions. I thought of philosopher Thomas Berry's comment that the future belongs not to those who have the most but to those who need the least. I bet Ely and Yos wouldn't agree. They only see the present. And in the present, the guy with the most toys wins. And they're not unique – given half a chance, there are precious few societies in the world where people would not opt for electricity and TV, motorcycles and access to a town.

We asked whether they had noticed a reduction in birds or fish or big mammals.

"Yes. There are fewer bird's nests to collect now," the two men told me.

"But why?"

"We collect the nests three or four times a year, so there are fewer swiflets, of course."

"What if you only collect nests twice a year? What if you set up some kind of control system?" I asked.

"Yes! *Sasi*," they said, referring to a traditional control of harvesting natural resources. But they gave me looks that said it would never work. "The problem is, if we don't take them, someone else will."

"Who?"

"Outsiders."

ARU HAS BEEN A COMMERCIAL HUB FOR CENTURIES. When the Victorian explorer Alfred Russel Wallace was here in the middle of the nineteenth century he wrote:

> The trade carried on at Dobbo [now Dobo, still the only town in Aru] is very considerable. This year there were fifteen large praus from Macassar [Makassar], and perhaps a hundred small boats from Ceram, Goram, and Ké [Kei]. The Macassar cargoes are worth about £1000 each, and the other boats take away perhaps about £3000 worth, so that the whole exports may be estimated at £18,000 per annum.

Then and now the town of Dobo flourished because traders were raping and pillaging what Wallace called "natural productions."

Dobo, where the majority of Aru's sixty-three thousand people live, is in the running for the most miserable town in Indonesia with stinking open drains, houses built over tidal flats reeking of sewage, muddy lanes, malarial mosquitoes, and surly, overfed Chinese traders. Half-hidden away in the back of restaurants we saw rare parrots and cockatoos, available for a price. We ogled baskets of turd-like dried sea cucumbers and piles of dried sharks' fins. Merchants happily offered to sell us trinkets made from mother of pearl whose real price was never mentioned – the environmental cost, of course, but more important the fact that the untrained village lads who were paid by the piece sometimes got the bends because they dove too deep or came up too quickly, using faulty equipment provided by the Chinese traders. Boats sailed from Dobo to Hong Kong restaurants with reef fish caught by dynamiting the coral beds. Other boats were loaded with live green sea turtles as long as a man's leg, stacked on their backs like grotesque poker chips. In the Aru village of Sia, we saw where many of these creatures came from. Friendly kids offered to sell us cassowary eggs, crocodile skins, and dugong teeth. I admired a small green parrot that a young happy boy offered, a bargain at only five dollars and protected by a law conceived in distant Jakarta. The boy had no concept this was an endangered species, a heritage of mankind, a treasure beyond words, a poster animal for the Western conservation movement. To him it was simply a product that could help him earn his school fees.

THE UNIVERSAL AXIOM IS THAT WHEREVER PEOPLE aren't in control of their resources, nature gets hammered. This is the essence of the conservation problem.

ONE DAY MARK AND I WANTED SOME VEGETABLES TO accompany the daily diet of roast pork and fish, and in the forest of Aru I asked Ely if there were any edible leaves growing nearby.

Ely disappeared for the afternoon. That night we were pleasantly surprised when he cooked up a potful of dark green leaves, probably thinking it doesn't take much to keep two Europeans happy. The next day, while out walking, we came upon a tree, maybe five meters tall and ten centimeters in diameter that had recently been chopped down. "What happened here?" we asked. "Yesterday you said you wanted vegetables," Ely answered, plucking some withering leaves from the fallen tree. We were incredulous. "Never mind," he said, allaying our unspoken doubts. "The deer like these leaves. We'll go hunting here tomorrow."

AROUND THE FIRE WE GOT TO TALKING ABOUT ABstractions.

"What's the most important thing to give to your children?"

"*Sayang*," Ely and Yos answered. Love and attention. "And education."

"Are you people more like the [Malay-race] Javanese or the [Negroid] Papuans?" I asked.

"Papuan," they agreed.

"I see lots of Javanese in the towns," I said, expecting to provoke an anti-Javanese response. "Javanese settlers move to West Papua for transmigration. Javanese run the government."

"We need more education," Ely and Yos answered warily.

"Why don't you have better schools?" I asked, recognizing I was treading on sensitive ground.

"The Javanese want to keep us stupid," they eventually said.

"And the future? What about your son, Ely? Will he grow up to be an engineer, or governor of the province?"

Ely and Yos were silent. I pushed. Is there an Arunese equivalent of the American dream in which any child can grow up to be president?

"The boy will probably grow up to be like me," Ely finally admitted.

"And his world?"

"More people. Too many people fishing with nets. Fewer fish, fewer turtles. Fewer birds of paradise."

Ely and Yos then asked me what I thought would happen to nature.

I felt strangely close to these men. I told them how they face the same problems as other rural people. How rich countries, like mine, could afford anything they wanted, and how less-rich countries, like theirs, survived by providing these luxuries. I told them about bird of paradise feathers being in demand a century ago for ladies' hats.

They were too poor to offer us tea.

We talked about the Indonesian concept of a *Ratu Adil*, a just leader. How local people, like Ely and Yos, know full well how to maintain wildlife populations but don't have a chance because the global marketplace forces them into rapidly depleting their birds nests. If Ely and Yos don't make money from nature, then someone else, an outsider, will. To me it was clear. Don't give outsiders a chance to get rich, I said. They listened quietly.

I thought I should tell them about UNPO, the Dutch-based Unrepresented Nations and Peoples Organization that fights for statehood for Mohawks from Quebec, Kurds from Iraq, and Frisians from Holland. And if that doesn't work, well, get tough.

Then I stopped. I sounded like a suburban Che Guevera. Like a college student of the late sixties. *Rebel. Get control of your destiny. Peasants of the world arise.* I was sounding ominously paternalistic, naively middle-class.

"Wouldn't you be happier being in control of your resources?" I asked. With each question Ely became increasingly withdrawn. To me the conversation was a mischievous intellectual exercise, like asking, during a spring afternoon on campus in 1968, whether we should take over the university president's office. To Ely, however, this talk was conspiratorial, vaguely illegal, and certainly antisocial, and not at all in the spirit of Indonesia's national feel-good philosophy of *pancasila*.

"Too bad we haven't seen birds of paradise," I said, changing the subject. Like many visitors, we longed to see these rare birds, found only in Aru and New Guinea and surrounding islands.

We accepted that we would never glimpse these rare

creatures, so instead we explored the island's caves. In one cave, up to our knees in cold water, our flashlights caught glimpses of spooky white fish, and we flailed around like schoolboys trying to catch some in our mist net, which was designed for nocturnal bats. Surely these albino fish were new to science. We'd become famous. Our idea was that we would catch one, pickle it in alcohol, and send it to an ichthyologist for identification. Too bad for the fish, but that's the price of science. Ely, seeing what we were after, borrowed one of our flashlights and disappeared into the depths of the grotto. He came back twenty minutes later with two small, pale fish that he had speared. OK, they were damaged, but an expert could still examine them. We were somewhat less amused when they arrived on our dinner plates a couple of hours later, grilled.

FINALLY, ON OUR LAST MORNING, ON THE WALK OUT of the forest we saw a tree full of birds of paradise. There were well over a dozen, their calls somewhere between a squawk and a honk, call it a squank. One male was displaying, yellow and white tail feathers splayed, like a Portofino playboy cruising in his Ferrari. This was the great bird of paradise, one of just two of its species found on Aru.

Timo, a Javanese who seemed to have no clear job description in our small expedition, gazed up at the birds and said he wished he had a gun. We thought this a bit odd since Timo works for the Indonesian Department of

Nature Conservation. We suggested that his department was supposed to conserve things. Our comments didn't seem to change his attitude, and he made irritating popping noises for the rest of the day.

But I wasn't about to let Timo shatter the moment. We gazed upward and watched the birds of paradise for half an hour. Mark and I remember this as a profound experience. Ely and Yos patiently waited until we had gazed our fill. Timo, realizing he couldn't shoot the birds in our presence, wandered about, bored. Funny, isn't it. Ely looked at the bird and saw a meal ticket, while Timo the game warden mentally calculated how much the birds would be worth stuffed and sold to a trader.

I tried for a final time to instigate Ely to revolt. "*You should be controlling these birds of paradise.*" As soon as I said it, we both knew it was unlikely. Without saying a word, Ely and I looked at Timo and then back at each other in understanding. Timo, who was not from there, nevertheless had access to this forest, and, via his government job, some authority that he could leverage into bribes in exchange for turning a blind eye to trading in birds of paradise. If push came to shove, it would be the Timos of the world who got control of the birds of paradise. I looked at Ely standing there in his shorts and carrying his bow and arrows and remembered our conversations about his needing money to send his son to school. I then looked up at these valuable birds, true things of beauty. It's easy to paraphrase Keats, I thought, if you can afford to carry a Nikon around your neck.

ARE LOCAL PEOPLE ALWAYS
GOOD STEWARDS OF NATURE?

Conventional wisdom, as implied in the story of Ely and Yos in Aru, is that indigenous people realize they are part of nature, take only what they need, leave enough for future generations, and respect the natural world in ways that non-indigenous people (usually white men, but increasingly local cousins with power) cannot.

The paradox, often ignored by conservationists, is that there are many examples of civilizations that were in control of their resources but that nevertheless decimated nature; in many cases indigenous people have been as rapacious and short-sighted as the modern men and women who destroy forests and wipe out wildlife.

Conservationist Jeffrey A. McNeely notes that some sixty thousand years ago, the first people arrived in Australia from Indonesia and relatively quickly hunted to extinction marsupial lions, giant wombats, giant kangaroos, and dozens of other species, leaving behind a diminished fauna that is now being replenished by exotic species such as camels, dogs, cats, foxes, and weasels.

Paul Martin, of the University of Arizona, has compiled data on the extinction of numerous large mammals from the Americas shortly following the arrival of the first humans, who traveled across the

Bering Sea toward the end of the last Ice Age some fourteen thousand years ago. These First Americans found an amazing wealth of mammoths, mastodons, horses, camels, saber-toothed tigers, dire wolves, giant ground sloths, lions, and many other animals that apparently were hunted to extinction within a few thousand years of the arrival of people. The so-called "overkill event" was so sudden that Martin has dubbed the episode as a "Blitzkrieg" or "lightning war."

More recently, when the first Polynesians arrived on the myriad islands that range between New Zealand to Hawaii, they found hundreds of species of flightless birds that had evolved in the absence of any mammals. Such birds, such as the moa in New Zealand, were easy pickings for the Polynesian hunters and were speeded on their way to extinction by the rats and pigs that arrived along with the people. The earliest Hawaiians found eighty-eight species of land birds when they arrived, but only forty-three were left when Captain Cook "discovered" the islands three hundred years later (only twenty-seven are left today).

The first settlers on Madagascar came from Indonesia fifteen hundred years ago and wiped out more than twenty species of mammals, including giant lemurs the size of gorillas. And deforestation was a factor in the demise of the civilization that created the famous monolithic stone statues of Easter Island.

The spiral that launched a village drama.

KILL MOSQUITOS 'TIL
THEY'RE DEAD

*Choreographing the horny goat, the cute twin rabbits,
and the singing chicken.*

JAKARTA

ncense is far from a simple commodity. It's an essential component of Indonesian meditation. But add a swig of insecticide, manufacture it into coils that emit an insect-defying smoke, and you get that wonderfully Asian invention dubbed the mosquito coil. Ridding the world of little devils, either through prayer or poisoning.

Back in the 1970s, Hennoch Tampi, one of the clients of the Jakarta advertising agency in which I worked, wanted a new campaign for his three mosquito coil brands. In the visual and not always literate marketplace, they were named after the animals represented on the packs: Kambing (Goat brand, so called because it has a picture of a goat on the front), Ayam (Chicken), and Dua Kelinci (Double Rabbit).

I felt I owed him a Big Idea. After all, he was the first to feed me rat curry, a major treat in his hometown of Manado.

We did lunch at the Executive Club.

"How about we get some famous comedians to slap each other all night because they can't sleep because there are so many mosquitoes because ..." he suggested.

I saw greatness beckoning. "Here's what we do," I said, scribbling on the linen tablecloth. "The film starts with an animated scene of a mosquito control tower sending mosquito fighter-plane warriors to attack a peaceful human village. Who comes to save them? I paused, like I imagine Steven Spielberg would during a film pitch. "Why the heroes of the mosquito war – Super Kambing, a human goat dressed like Superman but with horns; Abdul Ayam, a giant chicken looking like a refugee from Aladdin's lamp; and Titi and Tati, the two rabbits. Together they beat up the mosquitoes and save the village."

"Is that it?"

"Oh, I forgot. They sing." And I made up a jingle while gulping chocolate mousse.

He loved it so much he paid for lunch. Now I really owed him.

First I flew to Singapore and saw my buddy Horace Wee. Whenever I had a jingle idea, I sang it to Horace and he would grimace, strum on his guitar, and say, "surely *this* is what you had in mind." Without the aid of a synthesizer, he would then take the basic melody, call in a few of his musician friends (we were usually on a tight budget, and we'd get a couple of high school violin players to record, then overdub, time and again, the string parts, creating the impression of an orchestra), and make a demo reel of the jingle with a bossa nova beat, a soft jazz version, a bubble-gum pop rendition, a spirited march, and a Johnny Mathis-like soft ballad.

The film was combination live action and animation – the cartoon mosquito villains would be added later. I gave the role of Super Kambing, the goat superman, to my kung fu instructor, a Bruce Lee protegé. He asked that filming not interfere with his special armed forces assignment. "I'm bodyguard to the ambassador," he said.

"Which one?" I asked.

"Yours. The American."

His buddy was a perfect Abdul Ayam. We told him he looked very nice in his turban and balloon pants.

Now for Titi and Tati.

I liked to hold casting sessions in the office. It amused my colleagues to have wannabe commercial stars prancing around.

We found Titi, the first rabbit pretty easily. But no Tati, and we were on the fourth casting call and shooting was set to start in a few days. Then a beautiful Arabic-Indonesian lady arrived, a minor film actress, together with a friend.

"Can you do kung fu?" I asked the actress.

"No."

"Karate?"

"No. And I won't wear skin-colored tights."

"Well, then you must be able to dance."

Her eyes lit up. "Yes. Disco."

She didn't get the job. But the Arabic-Indonesian woman's friend, Yeti, was great. She had rabbit-like curves and had been a gymnast.

"Have you ever been in a film?" I asked.

"No, and I don't want to."

I looked her straight in the eyes with my most intense, but sincere, gaze. "Yeti," I said. "I can make you a star."

The shooting went smoothly. We had asked the prop man to get white smoke coming from the end of the fake two-and-a-half-meter mosquito coil. So before every take, he puffed on two packs of cigarettes and stuffed them into the hollow end of the model mosquito coil.

During the mosquito attack, a terrified mother clutching a baby looks up at the sky and implores, "Who can save us?" And we figured we'd have a great shot because the kid would be crying her eyes out. All little kids cry when they're put in front of the lights and surrounded by strangers. Well this mellow kid wouldn't stop laughing and gurgling. "THE MOSQUITOES ARE COMING! WE'RE DOOMED! SAVE US!" people screamed. "Gurgle, gurgle," continued the baby. "Go on Tony," I told the Australian director. "Pinch the kid."

"I can't," he answered. "I've got a kid her age. I hate to see little girls cry. You pinch her."

The two rabbits were terrific. They swung on vines and punished an imaginary giant mosquito with flying kicks.

There's one scene in the commercial in which a little old lady chases the fleeing mosquito villains with a broom. Of course there were no giant anthropomorphic mosquitoes for her to chase during the shoot since they were to be animated and added later.

"Now, Ibu, in this scene you're really angry," I explained. "You're chasing after these real bad mosquito villain guys." Here we were asking a four-toothed, seventy-something woman who had probably seen about two commercials in her life to give a performance that would have challenged Dame Judi Dench. "You can't really see the mosquitoes, Mother, but I want you to chase them down this path just the same. They're about this big," I said, holding my hand as high as her shoulder. "Pretend they're there." And she did, with gusto.

The grand finale of this epic comes after all the mosquitoes have been run out of town and the villagers cheer their four mosquito-banishing heroes. After the first take, Titi, Rabbit Number One, was furious. Some boys in the front row of celebrating villagers were, well, taking liberties. We moved the naughty boys to the back and the little old ladies to the front. Kambing the Goat picked up the baby and swung her over the crowd. The baby was supposed to be happy and gurgling, safe in the hands of the friendly giant who killed mosquitoes and saved the village. The formerly happy kid bawled and screamed. Never mind. It was a long shot, and with a bit of luck we wouldn't see her face. Film was expensive and the cast of dozens was getting restless.

"All right, you barnyard animals, SING!" Tony shouted.

"I'm Super Kambing," the goat man bellowed.

"I'm Abdul Ayam," the chicken crooned.

"We're Dua Kelinci," the rabbits trilled.

"And we've come to kill mosquitoes 'til they're dead."

Does this fish stir your soul?
Arnaz Erdmann diving with a coelacanth.

Photo: MV Erdmann

NEW SPECIES CAUSES GROWN MEN TO "TREMBLE WITH EXCITEMENT"

Discovery of the coelacanth in Sulawesi, and why some scientists get a headache when they find something new.

MANADO

t's hard to imagine what will stir a man's soul. For some it's a sports victory, for others a romantic encounter.

For Mark Erdmann it was a large, ugly fish that oughtn't to have been where it was.

He held an important new species in his hand and let it get away, making one of the biggest scientific blunders imaginable.

And then he got it back again.

Erdmann, 33, an American marine biologist working to develop marine-protected areas in the northern part of Indonesia's Sulawesi island, stumbled on one of the most significant prizes in marine biology, a coelacanth, a rare fish a continent away from where it was thought to belong.

The coelacanth ("SEE-la-kanth") is an ancient fish sometimes dubbed the "dinofish" because it was known only by fossil records and assumed to have gone extinct some seventy million years ago, about the same time the dinosaurs disappeared. When a fisherman caught a coelacanth in 1938 in the Indian Ocean north of Madagascar, the scientific world was stunned.

THE MEDIA HAS COINED THE TERM "LIVING FOSSIL" TO describe a living species thought to have evolved little through the ages. Several well-known examples are some forms of sharks, crocodiles, fresh-water turtles, opossums, aardvarks, and pelicans.

Slightly different is what scientists call a "Lazarus taxon," to describe a life form thought to have become extinct but that suddenly reappears, as if it had "come to life again." The coelacanth fits this description, as does a long-whiskered rat, thought to have been extinct for eleven million years, found in 2005 in Laos.

JUST DAYS AFTER THEIR WEDDING IN SEPTEMBER 1997, Erdmann and his wife Arnaz took four friends to the fish market in Manado, a city in northern Sulawesi. "We stepped out of the taxi and an old guy pushed a cart past us that contained a large fish," Erdmann recalls.

"My wife said, 'what in the world is that?' I recognized it as a coelacanth. Manado's a city of one million; it was like finding a dinosaur in Central Park. The fisherman didn't speak much Indonesian and he seemed uncomfortable, so I just took some photos and we each went our separate ways. It just didn't seem feasible, and I figured if it really was a coelacanth, we'd find another. Anyway, we didn't feel like dealing with a four-foot smelly fish in our hotel room."

Several days later, on the plane journey back to the States, Erdmann remarked to his wife that "maybe we should have bought that fish." He admits now, "I was the biggest bonehead ever."

Erdmann's friends put the coelacanth photo on the website they had created to share images of the wedding. "Within five hours someone called and said, 'get that coelacanth photo off the web before anyone else sees it.'" Erdmann saw the wisdom of not publicizing the discovery until conservation measures had been put in place to protect the rare creature. And anyway, the only proof he had was a photo. "Some other scientists called it a 'honeymoon hoax,'" Erdmann says.

Erdmann put out the word in the Manado fish market that he wanted to buy a coelacanth, and some ten months later a fisherman phoned Erdmann and subsequently sold him one, which the fishermen call "Rajah Laut" (King of the Sea), for around seventy dollars. (In November 1999, exploring in a small submarine, Erdmann and his colleagues found two more coelacanths in a volcanic cave on a steep rock face at a depth of one hundred fifty meters, similar habitat to where the African specimens were found.)

Erdmann sent the large fish, twice the length of a man's arm, to colleagues to verify it was, indeed, a coelacanth, but still didn't publish his discovery. Instead, Erdmann briefed top Indonesian officials, setting in place conservation measures that began when the discovery was published in the journal *Nature*.

Erdmann's fish turned out to be a different species to the African variety, *Latimeria chalumnae*; he named it *Latimeria menadoensis*. The two coelacanths are morphologically similar but differ genetically by five million years. He explained these fish are called "old fore legs" because of their characteristic dorsal fins. The coelacanths, which first appeared some 400 million years ago, branched off from the "normal" ray-finned fish at an early period. "Some people think they're precursors, along with lungfish, of sea animals that eventually became terrestrial," he says.

When Erdmann found the coelacanth, he had already discovered fourteen new species of mantis shrimp. Was this a different feeling?

"There is a unique euphoria in finding a new species and realizing that you are the first human to recognize this life form as something separate from all others – as if you've been privileged to a first showing of a new exhibit in the gallery of life."

NEW CREATURES ARE REGULARLY BEING DISCOVERED; in 2014 alone some eighteen thousand new species of plants and animals were identified. Some highlights of new species found in the last few decades: a new cat from an island between Japan and Taiwan, two new monkeys in Brazil and one from India, two new lemurs in Madagascar, three new deer in Vietnam, and a round-eared sengi, or elephant shrew, from Nambia, caught with traps laden with rolled oats, peanut butter, and Marmite. It's only mouse-sized, but nevertheless is a distant relative of its namesake animal. About a hundred of the roughly five hundred species of shark have been found only in the past decade. Plus numerous birds and more insects and amphibians than you can shake a stick at.

ALFRED RUSSEL WALLACE, A MID-NINETEENTH-CENTURY naturalist and beetle collector who roamed Southeast Asia for eight years, broke through Victorian emotional reticence to write about the passion of finding new species.

Wallace "trembled with excitement" at finding a new butterfly in Sulawesi, and almost swooned when he found a new bird-winged butterfly in Bacan, in the Moluccas, writing:

> ... none but a naturalist can understand the intense excitement I experienced when I at length captured it. On taking it out of my net and opening the glorious wings, my heart began to beat violently, the blood rushed to my head, and I felt much more like fainting than I have done when in apprehension of immediate death. I had a headache the rest of the day, so great

was the excitement produced by what will appear to most people a very inadequate cause.

He got downright poetic with yet another butterfly he captured on the island of Aru:

> It is true I had seen similar insects in cabinets, at home, but it is quite another thing to capture such one's self – to feel it struggling between one's fingers, and to gaze upon its fresh and living beauty, a bright gem shining out amid the silent gloom of a dark and tangled forest.

I find this curious, and thoroughly refreshing. Passion is an emotion, and therefore seemingly outside the realm of science. But enough scientists experience this state to give us pause.

When Charles Darwin discovered a new beetle, he wrote that "no poet ever felt more delighted at seeing his poem published than he had upon first seeing, in *Illustrations of British Insects*, the magic words, 'captured by C. Darwin, Esq.'"

Henry Walter Bates, who first introduced young Alfred Russel Wallace to the myriad joys of collecting insects, and who traveled with Wallace to the Amazon in the 1840s (where Bates developed the theory of mimicry), discovered a new *Callithea* butterfly. Bates was ecstatic when a now-forgotten entomologist in the British Museum (Natural History) named the creature *Callithea batesii*. Arnold Brackman, a Wallace biographer, wrote:

Bates had achieved a place in the sun, albeit a modest place, yet a place, the torque that turns all pathfinders, whether in jungle or on ice flow ... Ego? Ambition? The pursuit of immortality? An irrepressible thirst for the meaning of meaning? A combination of these? Whatever it was, this was the motivating force that drove Bates back into the horrors of the rain forest.

That seems to be part of the key. Part of the satisfaction of discovering a new species seems to come almost as a reward for enduring discomfort and loneliness.

I GOT A SMALL TASTE OF THAT PAIN-BEFORE-PLEASURE principle while searching for a bowerbird in the Arfak Mountains of West Papua, on the island of New Guinea.

I was chilled by a steady, cold rain, hungry after several hours of muddy trekking. I hauled myself up a steep, slippery hill, grabbing exposed roots for a handhold, in search of a glimpse of how another species gets the girl.

Unlike the brightly colored males of most species of birds, the male of the Vogelkop gardener bowerbird, a species found only east of the Wallace line, and only in the sharp-edged Arfak Mountains, is an unexciting brown with little sex appeal of his own. He needs to advertise.

Specifically, he builds a bower — a display area in which he can show the female he is courting that he is a worthy mate. His bower becomes the avian equivalent of a

Porsche or a ski chalet in Vail or an Armani suit – it does not reveal his inner beauty but it does get a useful message across pretty quickly: "I'm cool, I'm hot, come visit."

I stoically followed my guide, Hangei Ullo, who wore a Duran Duran T-shirt and a safety pin in his left ear (useful for removing thorns from his feet).

Near the top of a ridge, at about fourteen hundred meters, we found the bower of the Vogelkop gardener bowerbird, *Amblyornis inornatus* (Schlegel), a dramatic one-meter-tall, maypole-like construction of sticks and twigs. In front of the bower, on two flattened areas like the terraces of a California split-level condo, the bird had placed some fifty candy-apple-colored seeds, a pile of iridescent black beetle exoskeletons, a blue and white ABC battery case, and some yellow wool thread. Some observers have seen bowers displaying carefully laid out film containers, bottle tops, and a baseball cap.

The first European to see the extraordinary bower of this bird was Odoardo Beccari in 1872, so obviously neither Hangei nor I could take credit for this find. Nevertheless, I sensed a bit of the thrill of discovery that no doubt infects people far from home who find something new.

I WONDERED WHETHER THE COELACANTH/BEETLE/ butterfly/bowerbird buzz holds for plants.

I accompanied Max van Balgooy, a much-experienced field botanist, on a collecting trip to isolated Aru island in eastern Indonesia.

Max is a rather short, rather round, always-smiling man who has an encyclopedic knowledge of flora ranging from the plants of Tahiti to the flora of the Indian subcontinent, and has had his fair share of discoveries.

One afternoon he returned to our base camp beaming.

"What's up?" I asked.

"New species."

This gave me a start. "What is it?"

Max unpacked his collecting pack, showed me a plant he had pressed that was already beginning to shrivel in the heat, and opened his notebook.

"No. 6511. STRONGYLODON? liana, infl. caulifloris and on young twigs, small flowers and pods, flower orange, pods inflated, ripe dehiscent red/black. slide"

His shorthand-like notes didn't betray much emotion, and I asked him how he felt at the moment of discovery.

"It was pure luck that I found the Strongylodon – the genus was never recorded from here. I was very excited; I recognized it immediately and it almost made me jump up and down."

His feelings in one word?

"Ecstasy. I know *exactly* how Wallace felt. I don't think you can explain this kind of feeling to someone who is unfamiliar with biological exploration. It's something more than just satisfaction or just pleasure."

"Max, is it as good as sex?"

He thought a moment.

"I'd say it was comparable to very good sex ... and there's no disease."

A newly-hatched baby turtle encounters a turtle skull on Shiva's Beach. He made it to the sea safely, on his own steam. And then he began his own hero's journey.

LIFE AND DEATH ON
SHIVA'S BEACH

Is a turtle worth risking your life?

PULAU ENU, ARU ISLANDS

newly hatched green turtle wandered into my tent this evening, attracted perhaps by a lantern that the reptile thought was the reflection of the moon on the sea.

A few hours later I roam the beach on the windward side of this small island, closer to Australia than to the Indonesian capital of Jakarta, blown sand gritting my contact lenses, looking for the tractor-like tracks that indicate an adult meter-long turtle has visited the low dunes to lay her eggs.

It is a night with stars like I've rarely seen. I examine small piles of sand that mark where one of these green turtles has laid her eggs. But, perhaps in too much of a hurry, she has deposited eggs below the high-water line, where they are certain to become waterlogged and spoiled. I finally unearth her sixty fresh eggs, still slimy with turtle juices, and transplant them into another hole I dig a few meters beyond the reach of the high tide.

Yet amidst this exuberance of life I smell death. I wander the beach and, like a dung beetle, am drawn to the rotting carcasses and bleached skulls of turtles that had been slit open by fishermen desirous of the two hundred or so eggs in the reptile's egg cavity, fishermen either too impatient or too greedy to be satisfied with catching fifty or so eggs as they plop out during the normal cycle. The tasty turtle flesh has been left uneaten to rot; the only part used was the stomach, which makes a fine bait.

IT HAD BEEN AN EVENTFUL DAY.

Earlier, the research group I was with had been cruising a few hundred meters offshore and through binoculars noticed a pile of upside-down turtles on the beach. Perhaps half a kilometer away, and about a hundred meters offshore, we also saw the boat used by the turtle poachers. We could see that it was full of live turtles, all upside down so they wouldn't move, perhaps a hundred of the animals, all destined for the meat market in Bali.

"Poachers," muttered Fata, an Indonesian game warden. Quickly the situation started to resemble a cowboy movie. "You go chase the boat," Fata instructed. "I'll rescue the turtles," he said as he jumped into the warm water and swam to shore.

Another Western conservationist and I urged the Indonesian captain to give chase. We made a half-hearted attempt, but the captain's heart wasn't in it. "Those men are armed and dangerous," said a frustrated Ating Sumantri, who is in charge of the Indonesian government's efforts to conserve sea turtles. "We don't have any soldiers, no weapons."

We then turned to shore to pick up Fata, who was nowhere to be seen.

Minutes later Fata appeared from the bush and told his story.

He had turned over eight of the one-hundred-kilogram animals and watched them escape into the sea until three poachers, who had been resting some distance away, saw what he was doing and gave chase. The three poachers were armed with machete-like *parangs*. Fata was alone and had no weapon. He took shelter in the woods until the fishing boat we had chased came close to the island to pick up their crew members.

I admired Fata's bravery. And I was angered by the timid reaction of the Indonesian boat captain and the government's inability to provide adequate manpower and resources.

So that night, watching a newly hatched turtle poke his head out of the sand, I wondered. What *is* a turtle worth? Worth getting stabbed for? Worth shooting some-one for?

HOW IS IT THAT WE HUMAN BEINGS WILL TRAVEL halfway around the world and suffer physical discomfort in order to reach a beach where green turtles come ashore to lay their eggs? Why would we watch another creature's life cycle – laying and hatching – with such emotional intensity and intellectual curiosity? Why would it disturb us that others of our race – the Balinese in this case – enjoy eating this ancient reptile? Why do we have such protective thoughts about another species?

LATER, IN BALI, I WANTED TO KNOW JUST HOW IMPORTANT turtle meat is in that island's Shivaistic Hindu culture. This was not merely being environmentally or politically correct. It's also good conservation to understand what emotional and spiritual values lie behind what seems to outsiders to be senseless consumption – some eighteen thousand turtles a year, according to one estimate.

"Turtle meat adds something to our ceremonies," explained I.B. Pangdjaja, head of public relations at the Bali Governor's office.

"But it's not essential to the religious ceremony?" I asked.

"Like you eating turkey at Thanksgiving. Except it makes you strong."

Odd, isn't it. Transported thousands of kilometers to Bali for *satay*, or worse, slit open for their eggs, and left to die on the beach. And then, against all odds, life goes on – more turtles come ashore to lay their eggs. Because we happen to be on Pulau Enu on this particular night, the bad guys stay away, and just maybe tonight's crop of eggs will hatch. I call this contradictory place Shiva's beach. A beach of destruction and creation.

Shiva dances on a beach of skulls
Ecstatic
Life breathes below

I AWAKE AT DAWN THE FOLLOWING MORNING AND THE hatch is well underway. I watch a bunch of just-emerged turtles, shorter than my thumb, scamper like reptilian puppies to the sea. After they all reach the sea safely, I strip so I can wash off the sand and bathe in the limpid sea that has been baptised by just-born turtles. After my swim I walk back to the nest site and see a straggler turtle emerging from the quickly heating sand, half an hour behind his nest-mates. I follow his clumsy but determined flipper steps into the sea and swim with him for maybe thirty meters. He paddles aggressively, sticking his little head out of the water every four seconds. The water is clear and warm, free of hungry fish or crabs, the sky blue and free of birds of prey. The little fellow swims toward a group of seven fishing boats far offshore. "Stay away from people," I shout, but he doesn't listen. The sea is big, though, and perhaps he will pass his life free of hassle. Soon he finds his own course and paddles out of sight. A boy. He isn't going to listen to me. He doesn't really know where he is going, but he knows he has a journey to make. I wish him well, as much for my sake as for his.

It's around here, I know it is.

Illustration: *Travel and Leisure*

SEARCHING FOR ENIGMAS

It's everywhere, it's nowhere, it's dancing in three-quarter time.

PULAU VALSE PISANG

ome people with stardust in their eyes and too much red wine in their veins spend their lives searching for Atlantis or El Dorado. Other adventurers windsurf across the Pacific. Yet other men and women seek an elusive metaphor, like Peter Mathiessen's snow leopard.

I have a simpler quest. I'm looking for "Waltzing Banana Island."

"Waltzing Banana Island," or to put it in its correct Indonesian-French nomenclature, "Pulau Valse Pisang," is a tiny speck of land in far eastern Indonesia. My search for the island is devoid of socially redeeming value; I'm simply intrigued how it got its name. A misspelling of the Dutch "valsche," which would make it the "False Banana Island"? A secret hideaway for Carmen Miranda? An abundance of fruit trees, or a crescent shape? Or, more romantically, maybe it was named by French explorers aboard the

Astrolabe who charted eastern Indonesian waters in the mid-nineteenth century. Since the banana is a euphemism throughout Indonesia for the male sexual organ, perhaps the lonely French sailors found the local lovelies *très charmantes*, musically inclined and welcoming.

How did this quest begin?

Several years ago I was glancing at a map of eastern Indonesia and saw a rather large title for Pulau Valse Pisang. The land mass it related to was just a pin prick. Why such big type for such a tiny land mass? And why such a peculiar name?

There are certainly worse travel strategies than to visit places with evocative names that purr with history and incense: There's Sumatra, Java, and Borneo; Malacca, Mandalay, and Makassar; Pondicherry, Kathmandu, and Ayudhya. Not to mention the rivers: Ganges and Yangtze, Mahakam and Mekong.

And Pulau Valse Pisang.

But before I could see for myself, I had to find it.

First stop was London's Royal Geographical Society, where I pored over old maps and atlases. Some of the tattered Dutch charts listed the place with the French-inspired "valse." But confusingly, some of the English maps used the Dutch word "valsche." About fifty-fifty.

The most helpful source was the *Official Standard Names*

for Indonesia, which was published by the CIA in February 1968. This phone book-thick tome lists several Valse Pisang islands. The one I decided was *my* Dancing Banana island is at S 2° 08' - E 130° 54'.

This happens to be at the southern edge of a region known as Raja Ampat, a vast sea off the western coast of the island of New Guinea, dotted with islands and home to the world's richest coral reefs.

I inquired about live-aboard diving boats, but the boat operators said they didn't go specifically to my island and that if I wanted to make a special stop, I'd have to hire the entire boat for a ten-day cruise.

Then I heard about Misool Eco-Resort, a new dive-oriented hotel just an hour from the object of my quest.

With Marit Miners, one of the directors, I visited Fanfalap, a village of two hundred that claims jurisdiction over the islands. "Nope, our control doesn't include your island," Ahmad, the head of the village, patiently explained. "And no, we have no idea why it's called by that odd name."

But I had the coordinates and Marit organized a group dive to the island.

We got out the GPS and approached. But the CIA in its wisdom only listed the location to the minute, not to the second. Our boat arrived at the CIA coordinates. We were in the middle of the dark azure sea, about half a kilometer equidistant between two islands. The island to the north was the large and well-known Pulau Daram. The smaller, idyllic-appearing island to the south, about two hundred meters long, I decided, was my oceanic grail.

To celebrate, I dived into the water and was startled, then pleased, to see a hawksbill turtle swim by. It wasn't too large, about the size of a pizza. Turtles can be just turtles, but they can be omens and cosmic messengers, and in my semi-sunburned state I chose to believe that this reptile was gliding around for a purpose.

As I was swimming, I thought maybe the CIA-indicated location was correct, and the island was a covert CIA installation hidden deep below the surface, like a secret redoubt of a villain in a James Bond movie. After all, it was the CIA that provided the coordinates.

We went ashore and my island (by now I had become more than a little protective of it) was a delight, with three white sand beaches and palms. A fisherman was on the beach, taking a break, and I asked him what the name of the island was. "Pulau Pinang," he said, referring to the name of a common palm tree. And where was Pulau Valse Pisang? "Oh, that's far away. Really far."

Never mind. I had taken an executive decision that this island was the one, and I was happy. But just for a while.

Then I had another thought, triggered by the earlier turtle sighting.

Perhaps my Pulau Valse Pisang island is transient and therefore everywhere, sort of like an itinerant deity that enjoys creating geographical conundrums.

Indonesian culture and belief systems are what the anthropologists call syncretic. In a huge oversimplification, ancient Indonesians started with various forms of animism and mysticism; then, like a hoarder, they didn't throw anything away. The accumulative Indonesians added layers of Vedic traditions, then Hindu, then Buddhist, then Moslem, even notions of Christianity and the modern religions of nation-building and consumerism. From my viewpoint, the Hindu tradition is one of the most interesting. Hindu mythology recognizes that Kurma, the second avatar of Vishnu, was a celestial turtle who played an invaluable role in churning the sea of milk to produce the nectar of immortality (it's complicated). Perhaps my Dancing Banana Island continually swims the oceans on its sacred turtle, gracefully waving its flippers in three-quarter time.

ABOUT THE AUTHOR

Paul up a river in central Sulawesi with a couple of paddles but
not much sense of humor. This Sulawesi adventure generated a
case of malaria, innumerable close encounters with leeches, and a
greater appreciation of hot showers.

PAUL SPENCER SOCHACZEWSKI has written *Share Your
Journey*, *An Inordinate Fondness for Beetles*, *The Sultan and the
Mermaid Queen*, *Redheads*, *Soul of the Tiger* (co-authored
with Jeff McNeely), and other acclaimed books, along with
some six hundred bylined articles in leading international
publications. He has lived and worked in more than eighty
countries, including long stints in Southeast Asia.

Visit Paul at:
www.sochaczewski.com